BIARRI

AND

BASQUE COUNTRIES.

BY

COUNT HENRY RUSSELL,

MEMBER OF THE GEOGRAPHICAL AND GEOLOGICAL SOCIETIES OF FRANCE,
OF THE ALPINE CLUB AND SOCIÉTÉ RAMOND,
AUTHOR OF 'PAU AND THE PYRENEES,'
ETC., ETC.

With a Map.

1873.

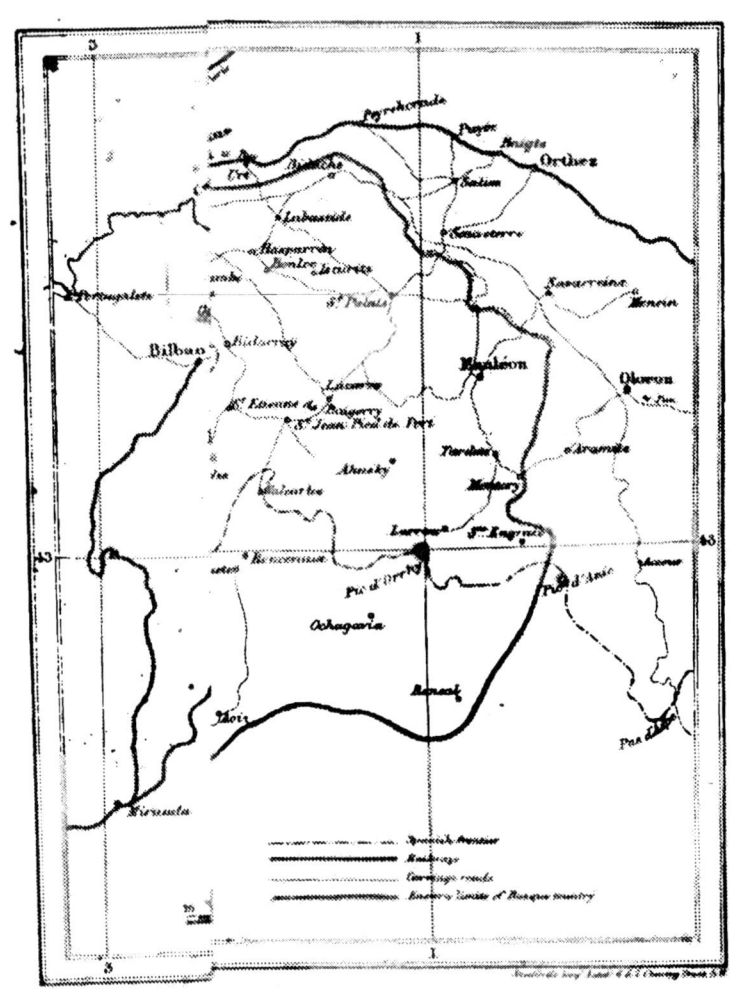

INTRODUCTION.

It is almost as difficult to guide a tourist as a lover or a sinner, when the country which the author attempts to describe is not yet popular and famous, and no one can be sure that what *he* loves or admires in it will have the same favour with those who do him the honour of following his steps or advice.

This is, however, what I have undertaken in these pages, conscientiously, but most capriciously written during my long walks through the wild and romantic Pyrenæan regions, called "Basque country," a land of mystery, whose mountains have not always a name, and whose immaculate torrents, like the sweet, but rash follies of youth, fling their glittering waves over every sort of precipice, always looking for a level, which they never find on land.

There are a few places, especially on the

Spanish side, which I had to describe without seeing them; but though I cannot agree with a witty author, who thinks this is often an advantage, my authorities for those places are too respectable not to be fearlessly accepted. They are: Adolphe Joanne's 'Itinéraire des Pyrénées,' Mr. Murray's always truthful 'Handbooks,' my young friend Henry O'Shea's 'Guide to Spain,' and Germond De la Vigne's little book on Biarritz.

I therefore hope and believe, although nothing human can be complete, that this Guide will meet most wants: and to British tourists who have a yacht I may also suggest a journey from England to Bayonne by sea, as yachts of all tonnage can enter its harbour, whence to Biarritz it is only five miles.

With these few words I leave the reader; for Guide-books are like friends: they can afford to be simple, as long as they are true, and need not look solemn.

H. R.

LONDON, *June*, 1873.

CONTENTS.

CHAPTER I.
Biarritz 1

CHAPTER II.
Bayonne 16

CHAPTER III.
The "Refuge" and the "Barre" 24

CHAPTER IV.
The Basques.—Their Origin, Migrations, Struggles, Territory, Population, etc., etc. 31

CHAPTER V.
The Basques 52

CHAPTER VI.
Basque Country 69

CHAPTER VII.
Cambo 75

Contents.

CHAPTER VIII.
St. Jean de Luz 86

CHAPTER IX.
Hendaye, Fuenterrabia, San Sebastian 95

CHAPTER X.
Dax, Buglose, and the Landes 109

CHAPTER XI.
Cap-Breton 116

CHAPTER XII.
Sare and its Caves 121

CHAPTER XIII.
Ascent of La Rhune (2920 Feet) 129

CHAPTER XIV.
Grotto of Isturitz 135

CHAPTER XV.
Bilbao 143

CHAPTER XVI.
A Riding or Walking Tour of about Ten Days in the French Basque Country 154

BIARRITZ AND BASQUE COUNTRIES.

PART I.

CHAPTER I.

BIARRITZ.

Biarritz is a charming village, fast becoming a small town, and pleasantly situated on a cliff of the Bay of Biscay, at about 20 miles northeast of the mouth of the river Bidassoa, where the Atlantic coast becomes Spanish, and suddenly begins to run from East to West. On a clear day, the immense curve of this line of coast, which is very mountainous in Spain, but quite flat in France, can be easily traced with the naked eye from any hill round Biarritz, for a distance of more than 100 miles, the last blue hills in the "far West" not being far from Bilbao.

Biarritz is little short of 500 miles (by rail) from Paris, 423 from Madrid, and 67 from Pau. By leaving London in the morning, you reach it the next day at one o'clock P.M. The railway station is two miles from the town, at *La Négresse*. (Omnibuses.)

A gayer little place it would be difficult to find, even in midwinter. Twenty-five years ago it was quite unknown, but now more than forty English or Spanish families reside there permanently; and in summer it suddenly becomes as crowded and elegant as a German watering-place. But its normal population is not quite 4000. It is capriciously and irregularly built, the houses looking as if they had fallen from the sky, the streets running up and down, right and left, but at almost every step letting you catch glimpses of the wild and blue ocean between two houses, or above them. It is the Bournemouth of the Bay of Biscay, but with the sun and colouring of Italy. There are trees in the streets—sycamores, tamarinds, &c. The walls are so white, that in summer their glare is as dazzling as snow. No streets are paved, so there is no rattling of carriages, and you hear no noise but the wind, of which there is plenty, to say the least. . . . It is indeed not like Pau in that respect.

It is far from easy to pass a fair judgment

upon the very changeable climate of Biarritz, as it varies not only during a given week or day, according to the wind, but sometimes from year to year, and to a strange extent. The contrast between its climate and that of Pau, which is barely 60 miles distant, is very striking. Whilst at Pau, which is so calm and tranquil, wind is almost unknown, the Biarritz atmosphere is as boisterous as any in Europe; and in favour of it, it must be admitted that the temperature is slightly higher than at Pau, especially in the evening and at night. It is well known that the ocean tends to equalize temperature. Snow is seen sometimes at Biarritz, but rarely; and when the south wind happens to blow, as it often does in the depth of winter, its burning blasts make the temperature run up to 70° (shade). The prevailing winds are from the west, south-west, and south, and they are by far the strongest. North and east winds (both very cold) blow but seldom. In clear weather the atmosphere is of such purity, that peaks fully 80 and 90 miles distant are seen to perfection with the naked eye; and from the top of the lighthouse the view extends from the Pic du Midi de Bigorre (E.S.E., 9439 feet) to Cape Machichaco, near Bilbao (W.); in all about 150 miles.

Nothing can be grander than an autumn sunset on the Bay of Biscay, seen from the Biarritz cliffs; the tints are both so warm and so angry, that sea and land seem on fire, and the clouds are awful to look at.

The ocean on this coast, where only two or three rivers can pollute it, is of the purest blue; it is never yellow or green. The temptation to bathe is therefore very great, and the water never being extremely cold, bathing is possible at all times of the year. But the surf is so great in autumn and winter, that the utmost prudence is required, since in fishing alone at least fifteen cases of drowning have taken place within the last three years, even at enormous heights above the sea.

There are three cold-bathing establishments, and a fourth for hot baths (Port Vieux). The sand on the beach, quite free from pebbles, is particularly fine and soft. It is also very porous, and dries up an hour or two after high water. The huge strand, which runs almost due north of the light-house, lined for 100 miles with green or dark pine forests, has all the strange splendour of a desert; and these pines do more than charm the eye; they are exceedingly useful in checking the advance of the sea, which used, before they were planted, to encroach on the land at an alarming rate every year, sweeping the sand-hills before it.

As for boating, it is seldom pleasant or safe on this terrible coast, and a ship is rarely seen on this angry wilderness of waters; still, a few sailing boats are to be had in the *Port des pêcheurs*, at the rate of 5 fr. for the first hour, and half that price for every succeeding hour.

There is a strange absence of sea-weed at Biarritz, and fish cannot be said to be very plentiful; the most common are tunny fish (often weighing 60 lbs.), soles, lobsters, and *dorades*. Countless multitudes of sardines are often caught a few miles farther south, and anchovies by millions, but seldom near Biarritz. Conger-eels are very abundant; they are caught at night, when they rise near the surface, and they are much relished by the natives of this coast.

HOTELS are many and splendid.

The *Hôtel d'Angleterre* (proprietor, M. Campagne) is a magnificent structure, 240 feet long, with twenty large saloons, bath-rooms and reading-room, a garden, interpreters for every European language, and commanding a most superb sea view. Strange to say, it was built in one year! The best Spanish wines can be had here, M. Campagne being also a wine merchant.

The *Grand Hôtel* (proprietor, M. Gardères) is also an enormous one, with the same view as the other. In both of these hotels there are *tables d'hôte* at all seasons.

The other hotels are: *des Ambassadeurs, de Paris et Londres, de l'Europe, des Princes.*

Villas abound, and are let furnished at any season. In summer prices are rather alarming; but the height of the bathing season only lasting two months, Biarritz may be said to be, for the rest of the year, as cheap a place (of its size and importance) as can still be found in Europe. During the winter it is eminently suited to small fortunes. There are numbers of houses (furnished), which can be had in spring and in winter for about 100 fr. *per month*, though during the season they fetch the same price *per day!!* (But for information on this subject apply to Victor Benquet, who keeps a public reading-room on the Place Ste. Eugénie; the best English and French papers, with a few Spanish ones, are always there, and a well-stocked lending-library.)

There is an English church, and a resident clergyman.

Biarritz also boasts of its *English Club* (near the Place Ste. Eugénie). The *Casino* is a wonderful place; but it only remains open for five months; and in winter its deserted terrace, swept by rain or hurricane, sadly reminds you of the lovely music and lovelier women who, a few months before, on warm autumn evenings, made you forget the splendid roar of the ocean, the hour, and every sorrow. It is a strange contrast indeed.

Still, even in winter, Biarritz is cheerful and lively. There are parties (dancing, dinners, &c.) at least twice a week. Several families entertain a good deal; and that the society of the place is increasing is proved by the graceful or sumptuous villas which are being built at both ends of the cliff, where the town extends in an undulating semicircle facing the west. On entering Biarritz by the north (as you come from Bayonne), you first behold on your right the Emperor's château, or *Villa Eugénie*, with its green fields and park (of which hereafter). On the other, or left side, you see an elegant villa, with slim turrets, now the property of the Duke of Frias. A little farther on, and on the same side, you come to a proud and imposing mansion, belonging to the Marquis de Javalquinto, which contains many fine pictures and other works of art. A few minutes after, you leave on your right a substantial, castellated building, the property of Mr. Bellairs, who also keeps a bank (*International* Bank). Just opposite (left) you pass *Sunny Side*, a most lovely villa of different styles, in which taste and imagination have accumulated and combined everything useful or beautiful in colouring and furniture. This exquisite gem is the creation and property of Mr. Henry O'Shea, author of the 'Guide to Spain.'

On the other, or southern side of the town, along the cliff commanding the whole Bay of Biscay, the visitor will first reach the *Villa Hamilton*, an Elizabethan house, built by Miss Hamilton, and visited by the Emperor. It is strikingly handsome, and the sea view from it is the best in Biarritz.

Close by, on the edge of the cliff, stands the lofty structure, built in the Basque style by the Countess of *Nadaillac*, as if to defy all the winds of heaven.

In the distance, on the wild and sandy beach which runs south towards Spain, the eye is attracted by a picturesque, Moorish-looking building, called *Marbella*. Lord Ernest Bruce owns it. It is a long mile from the town, has a glass dome of marvellous solidity, and a garden which makes it look like a refreshing oasis in a desert. The inside reminds one of the Alhambra court.

The *Goëland* must not be forgotten in a sketch of Biarritz. The view extends to every point of the compass, and it belongs to Count de Montebello.

Neither can we omit the *Bourguignon* house, with its charming garden, close to "Sunny Side." It was the property of a lady whom all loved and regret (Mrs. O'Shea).

Just beside the parish church (south-east of Biarritz) stands the *Grammont* château (M. Labat's), an imposing pile, with fine trees near it (a very rare ornament on this coast), and verdure all round. Napoleon III. spent two months there in 1854.

Lastly, near the light-house, and commanding all the country, the square house of the Marquis de *Noailles* looks from its cliff at half the Pyrenees and the boundless sea.

The VILLA EUGÉNIE, or Emperor's palace, is a very remarkable building, whatever architects may say of its faults. Its proportions and situation (to say nothing of the beautiful park, all created as if by magic, on a soil which used to look like the Sahara) make it exceedingly interesting, and certainly deserve admiration. It was begun in 1854, on the beach called *La plage des fous*, which runs north-east of the town towards the light-house. Two rocks, only 40 feet above high water, served as foundations: in fact, the spray is often blown over the whole of the terrace which extends before it. It is in the Doric style below, and Corinthian above.

It is open to the public on Mondays, from one o'clock until five.

The park (where 15,000 pines, six years old, were planted and thrive), the gardens and meadows, lake, &c., cover in all 30 English acres.

Do not forget to see the wonderful chapel built in the park, close to the Bayonne road. It looks Moorish, and glitters in the sun.

(*N.B.*—For all details concerning the Villa, see Ardoin's 'Souvenir de Biarritz.')

LIGHT-HOUSE.—It is certainly one of the curiosities of Biarritz, and well worth visiting, were it only for the panorama seen from the top.

Leaving the Bayonne road near the little chapel of the villa, you proceed to the left, gradually and gently ascending. After passing the *De Noailles* villa (left), look south-east, where the distant and snowy peaks of the Eaux-Bonnes, Cauterets, &c., begin to peer on the horizon, whilst the elegant light-house itself profiles just before you to the north-west, its snow-white column on the blue background of the gigantic ocean. It is just one mile from Biarritz.

You are allowed to enter, and, by giving a franc to the keeper, can ascend to its summit, until an hour before sunset. Its height (above its base) is 154 feet; but it is 220 feet from the mean level of the sea to the lantern, whose revolving light is seen at 16 nautical miles. No less than 256 steps lead up to it. The view is almost boundless, and the line of peaks from west to south-east is fully 150 miles in extent.

Here you are sure to see, in autumn and winter, even in the calmest and loveliest weather, such a stupendous swell as is never witnessed even on the west coast of Ireland. The mass, height, and length of these enormous waves are scarcely credible; they are hills of water, and their deafening roar is heard inland most distinctly at more than twenty miles! In fact, they make the coast tremble, and the rocks vibrate like bells. There is no place more treacherous than this for looking on or for fishing, as cataracts of sea water fly with the rapidity of lightning to an elevation where none could imagine he was not in safety; and ten or a dozen people have been drowned on this fatal headland within the last twelve years.

You can drive to the light-house by the road just described, and then walk back (at low water only) by the *Plage des fous* (S.W.) to the *Bains Napoléon*.

PORT DE REFUGE and PIER.—A wild scheme indeed, and which appears every day more and more hopeless. Napoleon III. suggested it, meaning to connect by a breakwater several of the detached rocks scattered on the north-western side of the *Port-Vieux*, and thus to form a small harbour, only open to the north. A clever engineer, M. Palaà, was entrusted with this almost superhuman undertaking: but the only result has been, after years of labour and more than one sacrifice of life, to accumulate a shapeless and useless mass of ruins along the intended harbour. The breakwater (or what is left of it) was built with concrete; artificial square blocks weighing 36 tons (some of them 48) were sunk by hundreds at random, and just where they liked to fall! But the tremendous surf has been playing with them, as if they were pebbles, and in 1868, one of them was carried right over the pier (22 feet above low-water mark) like a toy or a feather! For these, and for financial reasons, the works are now suspended. They have already cost 120,000*l*., and all to no purpose. In fact, nothing human can resist such a sea as the sea of

Biscaye, except, perhaps, at *St. Jean de Luz*, where nature has half made a harbour.

ATALAYA.—Here the view is also marvellous. It is a sharp promontory, with ruins on the top, and to the north of the *Port-Vieux*; the word itself, *Atalaya*, meaning an "observatory," in Arab or Spanish. The *Semaphor* is close by, being both a station for the weather observations, and (in winter) the telegraph office.

Numbers of houses in the Basque provinces, when built on a height, are called *Atalaya*. The insignificant ruins on the Biarritz Atalaya are those of a fortified castle, which stood there in the twelfth or thirteenth century, and was meant to defend the harbour, Biarritz being in those times still a great place for *whale fishing*. Later, however, the "monsters of the deep" emigrated to colder latitudes, where the Basques pursued them. It is very seldom now that a whale is found or stranded on this coast.

In summer and autumn, when the population of this little town is doubled or trebled, the rocks and beach are alive with gay crowds speaking almost every known language. Between fifteen and sixteen thousand foreigners visit Biarritz during the summer months, and the fall of the Empire has not in any way diminished the well-deserved prosperity of this cheerful and famous place, whose climate, in all seasons, is more and more appreciated. No doubt, it is cold sometimes, it *may* freeze for a whole week, but seldom more.* In general, it is very mild, the great July heats being tempered by an often strong sea-breeze. The rainy months are March, and sometimes April. Healthy people prefer the climate to that of Pau, but it is too bracing and too windy for consumptive persons. The sun is *always* hot.

DOCTORS.—Here are the names of the medical men now (1872) practising at Biarritz:—

English: Dr. Girdelstone.

French: MM. Adéma, Vicomte de Vauréal, Jaulerry, Affre.

---

* According to Dr. Ottley's comparative table of temperatures for 1863–4, it was generally about 4° (Fahr.) warmer at Biarritz than at Pau (in winter); but it rained less at Pau.

SHORT EXCURSIONS ONLY REQUIRING ONE DAY.

CHAPTER II.

BAYONNE.

It is five miles (by the high-road) from Biarritz to *Bayonne*, a handsome and wealthy town of nearly 27,000 inhabitants, situated on both banks of the river *Adour*, and four miles from its mouth. Within its walls the river *Nive* falls into the Adour. An omnibus starts from Biarritz every hour (in winter) for Bayonne, and every half-hour in summer. It is a pleasant drive of about 40 minutes, the road being lined, first with plane-trees, then with poplars, and passing (at the third kilomètre) before the gate of the charming and most fantastical *Villa Sophia*, belonging to M. Salvador, a Spanish gentleman. This villa is entirely "Moorish," and is covered with the most elegant arabesques.

A handsome bridge thrown over the Adour,

and made of stone, connects Bayonne with its suburb of *St. Esprit*, peopled mostly with Jews of Portuguese and Spanish origin, an intelligent and energetic colony, which settled there in the sixteenth century. The bridge is 840 feet long, and there are four other smaller ones on the Nive.

The Adour has its source in the Hautes-Pyrénées, at a height of 6000 feet, on the southern slopes of the *Pic du Midi de Bigorre*, and has a course of about 150 miles, but can scarcely be called navigable for more than about 40 miles above Bayonne. There used to be steamers from this city to *Dax*: but they have ceased to run, since the railway made them useless.

The Nive springs in the Basque country, and flows nearly due north for about 50 miles, before mixing its green and clear waters with those of the Adour in entering Bayonne. Bayonne to Pau by rail = 63 miles. There are three trains every day, both ways. Bayonne is a bishopric and a sous-préfecture; Pau, as the capital of the "département," being the "préfecture." And of all second-class *cathedrals*, Bayonne has probably the finest. It is its proudest building. This Gothic edifice, begun in 1141, and endowed in 1847 with an income of 1400*l*. a year by M. Lormand, has a magnificent altar of white Italian marble, and the sanctuary is paved with slabs of *blue* marble. The stained glass and organ are also both very remarkable.

The church of *St. André* has two graceful spires (Gothic).

Bayonne is, in some parts, rather gloomy, its streets being narrow and dark (a useful precaution taken against the fierce July sun), but it is very clean, has fine shops, and an unmistakable air of wealth about it, though its trade by sea has sadly declined for two reasons: first, the competition of the railway, and secondly, the slow, but sure and continual filling up of the *Barre*, or mouth of the Adour, where sand is accumulating to an extent daily more alarming, notwithstanding all precautions, and every effort to prevent it. It is indeed a sad prospect for this once flourishing sea-port. The *maximum* depth on the "Barre" is now under 20 feet, which is worse than unsafe, with a surf rising sometimes to twice that height!

Still, there *is* wealth in Bayonne, as the number of imposing country villas scattered all round it abundantly testifies. Its articles of trade are chiefly wines, Spanish wool, resinous matter, wood for building, &c. Its hams and chocolate are famous.

The *theatre* is a fine building. Behind it (west) extends a "place" where the garrison band plays on Thursdays and on Sundays; and here interesting observations may be made on the dress and features of the generally handsome inhabitants, whose Basque, "Gascon" or Spanish blood has engendered a mixed and most pleasing type of grace and manliness, seldom found united. The "grisettes" are nowhere so pretty. There is something "Andalusian" about them.

The British *Consulate* (— Graham, Esq.), is on the south side of this "place."

The *railway terminus* is on the right bank of the Adour, in the suburb of St. Esprit, where frowns the stern *citadel*, worth visiting for the view's sake, and in honour of the *Cimetière Anglais*, where were buried the 800 victims of the sanguinary sortie made in 1814. Bayonne only having opened its gates during the armistice, kept its proud motto, *nunquàm polluta*.

The history is most interesting. It is a very old city, and once belonged to the Romans, who called it *Lapurdum*, had a fleet there, and made it very strong. In fact ruins of Roman works are still found in it. Then it was plundered by the Normans, Visigoths, &c., finally lost its name itself, and became *Bayunna* (from *Baya ona*, two Basque words meaning "a good bay"). Later it passed (by the marriage of a Plantagenet with Eléonore de Guienne) into the hands of the British, and it was the last place (save Calais) which they possessed in France. Bayonne was retaken by the French in 1451, its governor and all the garrison becoming prisoners of war.

Vauban built the present citadel, and all the works now surrounding Bayonne, a "place forte" of the first class, however powerless it would certainly be against siege-guns of modern calibre. In fact every part of it is overtopped by hills, within range of large guns, and so useless is the fortified wall supposed to be, that it is likely to be soon demolished, the very dense population imprisoned within it having no longer room to move, and but little air to breathe.

Visitors limited as to time ought certainly to walk down the beautiful *Allées Marines*, on the left bank of the Adour. The trees, though cruelly mutilated in 1814, have now recovered all their original splendour, and for miles you can walk or drive in the shade, with the noble river on your right, and before you a conical and picturesque hillock, dark with pines, from the summit of which (three miles from Bayonne) the view, on sea and Pyrenees, is grand in the extreme. Just behind this hill are the ocean and the mouth of the Adour, or *Barre* (four miles from Bayonne), a perfect " hell " of roaring waves in bad weather. Opposite is *Boucaut* (right bank).

(For the road from the *Barre* to Biarritz, see Chap. III.)

It was in these angry waters that in 1814 eight British boats perished with almost all their crews, in entering the Adour. (See Napier, book xxiv., chap. 2.)

The mouth of the Adour has often been displaced. In the thirteenth century, it was at *Cap-Breton* (12 miles farther north, see Chap. XV.). In the following century it seems to have .been 12 miles farther still to the north. A great storm in the sixteenth century forced back the stream into its old channel.

There are steamers now and then, from Bayonne to the Spanish coast (to Bilbao, San Sebastian, &c. The office is quite near the British consulate), and occasionally to Monte Video, where the Basques emigrate in such vast quantities. Cod-fishing in Newfoundland is still kept up by Bayonne sailors.

HOTELS: St. Etienne, du Commerce, de la Providencia, des Ambassadeurs, &c.

DILIGENCES daily to all the Basque country: some start from the Hôtel des Basques (near St. André), others from the *Porte d'Espagne* (south of the town). But they are very bad. The diligence " service " to Pampeluna by the *Port de Maya* (south-east of La Rhune, 63 miles,) was stopped when the railway by San Sebastian was completed: still they do run sometimes, but irregularly.

No Englishman crossing Bayonne will fail to give at least a glance at the splendid mansion which, from the hill on the other side of the Adour, makes every building in the country look small. It is Lord Howden's house, called *Caradoc*, and large as a palace, containing many art treasures, and commanding a splendid view which it is impossible to describe.

For the battles on the banks of the *Nive*, south-east of Bayonne (Dec., 1813), see Napier, book xxiii., chap. 2. In five days' fighting the French lost 6000 men, and the allies upwards of 5000, five English generals being wounded.

The brave English soldiers who fell in the furious sally from Bayonne (April, 1814), are buried in the *Cimetière Anglais*, near the citadel. This sortie cost the French 900 men and one general; the British and German loss amounted to 830 men. (See Napier, book xxiv., chap. 5.)

CHAPTER III.

THE "REFUGE" AND THE "BARRE."

It is a little less than five miles from Biarritz to the "Barre," or mouth of the Adour (N.E.). You can either follow the long, straight beach, north-east of the light-house, and walk three tiresome miles on sand, or else take the carriage road, leaving the light-house on your left. Here on the cliff if the traveller look south-east on a clear day he will see 80 or 90 miles of peaks. At half a mile beyond the light-house the main road turns to the right, near a pretty chapel, and a sandy cart-road on the left leads, in ten minutes, to the once romantic "*chambre d'amour*," an ugly hole, now half filled with sand, where two lovers were once overtaken by the sea, never to be heard of again. (Maidenhair fern.)

There are small inns close to the "chambre d'amour," and bathing-houses on the beach.

At a mile beyond the light-house (two from Biarritz) you come to a sort of village, or group of scattered houses, called *Cinq Cantons*. Here, on a triangular "place," with a pretty kiosk on the left, the road divides; take the left branch, the right one leading (two short miles) to *Anglet*, on the Bayonne and Biarritz road.

After a few minutes you will observe on your right a pile of buildings, with the blue Pyrenees far away behind. This is the *Refuge*, always open to visitors. It is barely two miles and a half from Biarritz. Here were the head-quarters of Wellington in 1814. Founded in 1839 by the Abbé Cestac, a most zealous and venerable priest of Bayonne, this pious community of penitent women has succeeded beyond all hope, materially as well as morally speaking, for the wild plateau of barren sand bought by the abbé has become, in his hands and under his careful direction, the most fertile land in the country. All Biarritz has tasted the milk and the butter of the "Refuge." A beautiful kind of embroidery is also made here. (See Lawlor's 'Pilgrimages in the Pyrenees and Landes.')

The road continues north, leaving the Refuge on the right, and soon divides, on entering a dismal pine-wood. The right branch leads to Bayonne, crossing a strange region of pines and sand-hills (*dunes de Montbrun*), a solemn solitude, where no noise is heard but the moan of the wind and the roar of the sea behind, falling in cataracts on the distant and empty beach with a kind of metallic sound. If you follow *this* road (*Montbrun*), thus giving up the *Barre*, which remains to your left, you reach the top of a sand-hill, with a grand view of the Pyrenees in the south-east. Close by, on your left, quite hidden under the trees and lost amongst the sands, is a convent of *Bernardines*, nuns recruited partly from the "Refuge," whose whole life is spent in the culture of this sort of desert and in prayer. It is a very severe order; they never speak, and walk barefooted. They might be taken for ghosts, and their holy abode is silent as the North Pole.

Shortly after passing on the right of this convent (which you do not see) the *Montbrun* road descends, and finally meets the left bank of the Adour, just at the end of the *Allées Marines*, at a distance of four miles and a half from Biarritz, and one mile and a half from

Bayonne. By Montbrun it is therefore six miles between these two places.

But if you wish to see the *Barre*, you must follow straight on (north) when you enter the pine-wood. Two good miles from here (not five from Biarritz) will take you to the *Barre*, where the Adour rushes into the sea. There is a small light-house, and a long latticed pier (made of wood), meant to deepen the main channel of the river, by straightening it, and thus accelerating the current; but nothing will avail; the sand is accumulating every day, and only ships of very small tonnage can now make their way to Bayonne.

From the Barre to Bayonne is four miles, always on the left bank of the river. From Biarritz to Bayonne, passing by the Barre, it is therefore a little under nine miles. You can drive the whole distance, and through Montbrun also.

BOIS DE BOULOGNE.

This little tour of not quite five miles in all is very attractive, and may be taken in a carriage.

Leaving Biarritz by the parish church (half a mile south-east), you follow the main road to the railway station : but before reaching it, on entering a pine-wood, you must turn sharply to the right (west), and leaving on your left both the Madrid railway and a deep lake or pond (*Lac Mouriscot*), whose blue waters glitter beautifully on sunny days, you plunge into a wood of oaks, cork trees, and tall pines, where for a few minutes you might imagine you were crossing Canadian solitudes. It is a most romantic spot, and pretty wild flowers abound. On the lake there are boats for hire, for in spite of the coldness of its waters, there is plenty of fish in them. Subterranean communications are supposed to exist between this lake and two others, described hereafter (see p. 29).

On the hills opposite, behind the railway, there were fierce engagements in 1813.

The wood on this side (north) of the lake is so sheltered that it scarcely loses its leaves. The road now gradually turns to the right, towards the sea, between which and the Lac Mouriscot Napoleon I. once thought of digging a canal, navigable to men-of-war!

At last you completely turn round, facing the north, and leaving on your left the very beautiful château of *Marbella* (Lord Ernest Bruce), you re-enter Biarritz by its southern side and cliffs.

LAKES BRINDOS AND MARION.

They are both very small, and the former (*Brindos*) has shores as wild and dismal as can be seen or imagined. But lake *Marion* is surrounded with trees, and in summer its green banks are cool and pleasant.

The walk to both these lakes is about five miles in all, going and returning.

First go to the Biarritz railway station (two miles), or rather, go near it; but before reaching it you turn to your left, on the Bayonne and Madrid road, which you follow for about half a mile. You then leave it, turning to the right on a generally very muddy footpath. In ten minutes (on foot or riding), you reach the boggy shores of lake *Brindos* (only a few acres), a deserted and silent sheet of water, on whose brown and barren banks scarcely a tree is to be seen.

After a few minutes of melancholy contemplation, you will be too happy to leave it, and to retrace your steps towards the Bayonne and Madrid road, where you will return a quarter of a mile towards the station, and soon find a pretty carriage-road branching off to the right (N.W.). This will take you in ten minutes to the sheltered and green basin where the waters of lake *Marion*, protected from the wind, reflect their banks like a looking-glass. They are as calm and transparent as the eyes of a girl of seventeen summers.

Follow the north side of it, and in a few minutes (half a mile) you meet again the road by which you started, at a mile south-east of Biarritz, between the parish church and the railway station, and quite close to the former. (You can drive the whole distance, with the exception of half a mile, before coming to lake Brindos.)

N.B.—Most of the following excursions being through Basque territory, we had better devote a few chapters to a general description of this strange land and race.

CHAPTER IV.

N.B.—The whole of this chapter is translated from a French manuscript, kindly placed at my disposal and written by the Rev.—— Haristoy, parish priest of Sauguis, near Tardets.

THE BASQUES.—THEIR ORIGIN, MIGRATIONS, STRUGGLES, TERRITORY, POPULATION, &c. &c.

THE Iberians, both those of the Euxine and those of Spain (whether the latter descended from the former, or the former from the latter, *sive hi ex illis, sive illi ex his oriundi sint*, Menoch., Genesis, chap. x., v. 2) descended, according to the most learned historians, both religious and profane, from *Thubal*, the fifth son of Japheth, who was himselft he third son of Noah.

Authors are unanimous in fixing the time of their arrival in Spain, or in *Sethubalia* (which in Basque means "land of the sons of Thubal"), as early at least as the fifteenth century before the Christian era, since the Phenicians, who at that time penetrated into the peninsula, found them already established there.

Now, ancient authors, as well as modern ones, like Oyhenart, G. de Humboldt, Ampère, Amédée Thierry, &c., consider the Iberians as the ancestors of the Vasco-Cantabrians. The primitive names of several towns in Bethica (now Andalusia) have Basque etymologies perfectly justified by the topographical position (present or past) of those towns. As M. de Montglave has properly observed, the words or names of "Ararat," "Armenia," "Sinai," "Sem," "Bethulia," "Phasga," &c., mean "there," "close by," "oath," "son," "full of flies," "pasture land," &c., &c. M. Mentelle also tells us in his 'Dictionary of Ancient Geography,' that "the *Cantabrai* s a river of India, which Pliny counts among the most considerable which fall into the Indus." These different places therefore seem to show us the successive stopping places in the migration of the Vasco-Cantabrians, from east to west.

Pushed back by the Phenicians and Celts, by Rhodian and Phocean colonies, the Vasco-Cantabrians probably settled in that part of

Spain called later by the Romans *Taragonensis*, in the regions which have now become the provinces of Asturia, part of Old Castille, of Guipuscoa, Biscaye, and Navarre, and the northern districts of Aragon and Catalonia. (Diodorus of Sicily, Silius-Halicus, Ethicus, cosmography, &c.)

The above-mentioned authors, and likewise the geographer Strabo, Pliny, &c., give us interesting details about the customs, bravery, and countries of the Vasco-Cantabrians. Roman history shows them to us struggling with the Carthaginians, with the Romans also, for more than two centuries; and neither armies of the two great rival cities ever succeeded in reaching the interior or heart of Cantabria; for in spite of the verses of the servile Roman poet (Horace) who, although admitting the Cantabrians were unconquerable "before that time," *Cantaber non antè domabilis*, attributes to the Emperor Augustus the glory of having subjugated them, the Cantabrians were neither beaten nor submissive. In proof of which Tiberius, son-in-law and successor of Augustus (A.D. 14), was obliged, in order to secure their alliance, to promise to respect their institutions, and their autonomy. Vespasian also granted all the Cantabrians the right of *Latium*, and Caracalla that of Roman citizenship.

The Vasco-Cantabrians did not remain on the southern side alone of the Pyrenees; they made a passage for themselves through the immense forests of that chain, by a conflagration mentioned with the exaggeration characteristic of Greek authors (Diodorus of Sicily, and Denysius of Halycarnassus). Several names of Pyrenæan localities remind us of this conflagration; and those of Illiberris, Elusaberris (Eause), Bigorra (capital of the Bigorrians, *Bigorrienses*), Elimberris or Ilumberris (capital of the *Auscorrum*), &c., are indicative of unquestionably Basque etymologies. That is why Amédée Thierry, after Humboldt, &c., does not hesitate to affirm that "the most ancient monuments of geography show us the Iberian race occupying the great isthmus made by Gaul between the Gulf of Gascony [*] and the Mediterranean. The arrival of the

---

[*] It is well known that Strabo called the Gulf of Gascony Cantabrian Ocean (*Oceanus Cantabricus*), and de Marca calls it the *Basque Sea*.

first tribes of Gauls pushed back the Iberians towards the south; but the topographical names, such as are found in old Spain, prove the long stay, on the south side of the *Garonne* and almost as far as the Loire, of a population speaking the Iberian idiom, of which the present *Basque* language is a still living remnant."

Cæsar and other ancient writers had observed the analogies of language and customs which existed between the Cis-Pyrenæan and the Trans-Pyrenæan inhabitants, as also the differences existing between them and the Gauls, the Celts, and the Belgians.

These *Vasco-Cantabrians* of *Aquitania* followed Hannibal at Trasimene, at Cannes, &c. They defended their country against the invasions of the Cimbri and the Teutons. They fought beside their Trans-Pyrenæan brothers against the Romans under Sertorius, &c. When helped by their ultra-Pyrenæan brothers (for the dangers threatening the Cantabrian confederation always united them), they had to fight against the Roman legions commanded by Crassus, lieutenant of Cæsar; the *Venearni*, the *Monensi* (Moneins), the *Osquidates* (of

Ossau), the *Illuros* (Oloron), the *Sybillates* (Soule), spoken of by Pliny, are not mentioned amongst the people who sent their submission and gave up their hostages to the young lieutenant, then the master of Northern Novempopulania. On the contrary, Cæsar tells us that "a few petty people higher up in the mountains, *paucæ ultimæ nationes*, did not make their submission, and sent no hostages, being emboldened by the advanced season and the approach of winter." It is no doubt proved that the Cis-Pyrenæan Vasco-Cantabrians, when they saw their brothers beyond the mountains entering into an alliance with the Romans, towards the time of Tiberius, did admit *de jure* the Roman domination, for there was a Roman cohort at Lapurdunum, &c. (Bayonne). (The word Laphurdunum is Basque, and means "land of briars and water." In fact, formerly all the plains of Labourd, like those of Soule and of the Pyrenees, were lakes or morasses, and there are proofs of it.) But it is equally proved that the Vasco-Cantabrians on both sides of the Pyrenees *have always lived* (and under all dominations) according to their *fueros*, or old customs: the ultra-Pyrenæan ones until 1841 (for the privileges which they enjoy now are but remnants of their ancient *fueros*), and the others until 1789.

The Vandals, Herules, the Alains, the Suèves, &c., who came towards the year 409 from the banks of the Rhine, did not penetrate into the Vasco-Cantabrian country, neither did the Visigoths. The Franks of Clovis did not reach lower Novem-populania, consequently not our present countries. On the contrary, the ultra-Pyrenæan Vasco-Cantabrians, who had already made several descents upon the Adour basin, themselves pressed by the Visigoths in the Alava country and its neighbourhood (*Navarre*, "land of valleys"), tried to profit by the quarrels of Clotaire II. with Théodoret and Thierry, kings of Austrasia and of Burgundy. They therefore came down from their mountains, and joining their Cis-Pyrenæan brothers, they carried their conquests as far as the Garonne. (Frédégaire, chap. xxi., 54.)

What must explain the rapidity of these conquests was that the Gallo-Romans of Novem-populania were first enervated by the softening civilization which the victor's policy had inoculated, and then tired of the vexations and oppressions of the "masters of the palace," chiefs of the second race of our kings. To those times must be traced back those entrenched camps known under the name of *Casteras*, or *Touronac*, which are found in our countries and in lower Novem-populania. It is by mistake they are attributed to the Romans, whose camps differed widely from these.

The Vasco-Cantabrians did not at once settle down in the invaded territories as an homogeneous nation, when with their families they brought their laws, their customs, and language. They made sure their conquests far into Novem-populania, whose inhabitants had no difficulty in accepting and admitting the supremacy of the Duke of the Vascons. They strengthened their conquests by garrisons, by *Basque colonies*, organized in militia forces. Proofs of this can be found both in those entrenched camps and in the names, plainly and exclusively *Basque*, of several places in Novem-populania. For instance, Harriet, Biscaross, Itchous, Auzour, Arsa, Arrion, &c., &c.

(These names are taken amongst many, and literally, from a map of the Government of Guienne and Gascony, printed in 1700, by H. Gaillot, geographer to the king.)

Their conquests once made sure, the Vasco-Cantabrians established themselves as an homogeneous nation behind the line of *Aramitz* (*Ara-Ametz*), *Oloron* (Il-ur-on, "city of good water"), *Naverreinx* (Nava-erri), and *Sunarte* (Sauveterre). It is behind this line that they principally fortified themselves, and that we see them stand invincible against the armies of the Carlovingian kings. The new-comers settled especially in unclaimed lands between Labourd and Soule, which, in memory of the original country of its inhabitants, was called Basse-*Navarre*. Novem-populania, which after the name of the conquerors of the seventh century had been called *Vasconia*, preserved that name even after the retreat of the Basque colonies, flying before the armies of the second race of kings, towards the mountains, and behind the above-mentioned line. Just as beyond the Adour the *patois roman* changed the word *Vasconia* into *Gascogne*, and as *G*uillaume came from *W*illelmus, so among the Basques the name of *Vasconia* was changed into that of *Basconia*, from the habit of pronouncing V like B, which made the witty Scalier say: "Felices populi quibus *vivere* est *bibere*."

FRENCH BASQUE COUNTRY.

It is formed by three distinct provinces or "cantons": the western one is called *Labourd*, the eastern one *Soule*, and the central one *Basse-Navarre*. Formerly, as we said above, it was limited on the north by the Adour, on the south by the Pyrenees, on the west by the ocean, and on the east by the line which from Aramitz, passing through Oloron, Navarreinx, Suñarté, Sauveterre, went to meet the Adour. At a later period, whether on account of encroachments by the Béarnais, or because the Basques retired, the territory occupied by the latter was curtailed on the east. Moreover, as both the French and the Spanish governments are bent upon the eradication of the Basque tongue, the circle within which it is spoken is getting daily more limited.

Here are *exactly* the limits of the *French* Basque country, in other words, a list of the last villages beyond which the language spoken is the *patois* of Béarn or Gascony. Basque is spoken in the under-mentioned villages, going from west to east: Bidart, St. Pierre, d'Irube, Lahonce, Urcuit.

From north to south: Bardos, Ayherre, Orègue, Charitte-Alixe, Ilharre, Arbouet, Sussaute, Arbérats, Etcharry, Arouë, Charitte-le-bas, Arrast, Larrory, Mendibieu, Hôpital St. Blaise, Esquille, Haux, Ste. Engrace.

Biarritz and Bayonne were formerly Basque towns, as the name *Bi-Arritz* ("two rocks") proves it for the first; as to the second, its original name of Lapurduna, *Lapa-Ur-Duna* (meaning "a pool"), or *Lapar-Ur-Duna* ("land of briars and water"), and its second name of Bayonne, given to it towards 1132, *Baia-Ona* ("good bay"), prove it clearly, even if we had not also the authority of Esteban de Garibay (*Compendio historial d'España*), book iv. chap. iv. It must be observed that the Bay of Bayonne was better than now, when the Adour used to fall into the sea *near* Cap-Breton.

As to the village of *Anglet*, it is recent, and owes its name to a military post created there by the English when they possessed Guienne.

The French Basque country is formed by four valleys, having each its river, which crosses it in a direction perpendicular to the great mountain chain from which they descend. The most westerly of these rivers, the *Petite Nive*, or *Nivelle*, flows through the Labourd country, and meets the sea at St. Jean de Luz. The second is the *Nive*, and the third the *Bidouze*, which both fall into the Adour, the first at Bayonne, and the second near Guiche. . . . . The fourth river of the French Basque country is the *Saison*, which crosses the Soule country, and falls into the Gave of Oloron, near Sauveterre.

The three provinces of Labourd, Basse-Navarre, and Soule, had until 1789 their "general assemblies," or "states," and customs peculiar to themselves.

According to the last census, the *genuine* population of the French Basque country does not exceed, in all, 120,000 souls. There are 47,000 in Labourd, 46,000 in Basse-Navarre, and 27,000 in Soule.

SPANISH BASQUE COUNTRIES.

1. NAVARRA (*Nava-erri*, "land of valleys"), having Pampeluna for capital, has a population of about 300,000 souls. The kingdom of that name, founded in the ninth century, successively passed, through female descent, since 1234, into the hands of the houses of Evreux, of Aragon, of Foix, and lastly of Albret. It was usurped in 1512 by Ferdinand, King of Aragon, from the house of Albret, which only kept the *Mérindad* of St. Jean Pied de Port.

The chief towns are Pampeluna, Tudela, Olite, Estella, *Sanguera*, the town of St. Francis Xavier, apostle of the Indies. The father of this great saint was from Iatxou, near St. Jean Pied de Port (Basse-Navarre).

2. BISCAYA, having for capital Bilbao. Population of the province, about 130,000 souls. Bilboa (or Belvao) was built in 1300 by a prince of Biscaya, on the banks of the river called in Basque *Ibaïçabal* ("wide river"), or in Spanish, Nervion. The ancients called this river *Chabyls*. Its water was famous for the tempering of arms. That is

why the *Cantabrians* thought nothing of the arms whose iron had not been tempered in the Chabyls.

Bilbao lies in a fertile plain. The chief towns on the coast are *Bermeo*, or Bermejo, with a good harbour, and famous oranges. *Portugalete*, on the banks of a river. *Larédo*, built by the Goths, on a height surrounded on all sides by rocks, with a harbour below the town. *San Antonio*, with a harbour also.

The inland towns are *Durango*, in a deep valley, between lofty mountains: its inhabitants excel in working iron. *Hellorio*, in a pleasant and fertile valley. Its halberds were much esteemed, and its inhabitants still work iron most ingeniously. *Ordugna*, in a beautiful valley, everywhere encircled by steep and high mountains. *Lanestosa*, in a very similar position.

3. Guipuzcoa; capital, *Tolosa*. Population of the province, about 130,000 souls. Tolosa lies in a pretty valley, at the junction of two rivers, the Araxe and the Oria.

The chief seaport towns are: *Fontarabia* (*Fons rabidus*, or *Ocaso*, in Latin), built in amphitheatre on the slope of a hill; besieged by the French in 1638. *Irun* ("good town," in Basque), with a handsome church. *Renteria*, a picturesque village. *Passage*, a small town opposite the village of *Lesso*. *San Sebastian*, a city of pleasure and good living. *Gueteria*, built on a hill, birth-place of John Sebastian del Cano, who was the first to go round the globe, after three years' navigation. The Emperor Charles V. gave him as an armory, a globe with this inscription: *Tu primero me rodeaste*. *Zumaia, Deva*, formerly important in the times of whale fishing. *Motrio*, &c.

The chief inland places are: *Villafranca* and *Segura*, two handsome towns on the banks of the Oria. *Mondagron*, famous for its medicinal waters. *Placencia*, on the smiling banks of the *Deva*, and known for its fabrication of war weapons. *Bergara*, called the "shop of Mars." *Azpeïtia*, in a very pretty valley, containing within its territory *Loyola* and *Onis*, which both belonged to the family of St. Ignatius of Loyola. See the convent or house of St. Ignatius. Lastly, *Heybar* and *Helgoybar*, owing their importance to gun foundries.

4. ALAVA; capital, *Vittoria*. Population of the province, about 86,000 souls. Vittoria was founded by Sanche, King of Navarre, in a very fine and rich valley.

The chief towns of this province are: *Trevigno*, perched on a hill; *Pena Cerrada*, lying between very high mountains, &c.

The three sister Basque provinces, after having had their own lords till the thirteenth century, gave themselves up to the Kings of Castille, accepting them as their masters.

AMUSEMENTS OF THE BASQUES.

1. *Pastorals* or *tragedies*. The Basque language possesses about forty tragedies or pastorals, borrowed from the Bible, from mythology, from ecclesiastical or profane history. They are acted in the public squares, by young or even old men, in costumes, and very numerously attended. These compositions, full of stirring scenes, which M. de Montglave has compared to the comedies and tragedies of Aristophanes and of Sophocles, are far indeed from being the creations of poets " who knew neither how to read or write." The authors

of many of them are well known, and we believe their origin cannot be traced back beyond the fifteenth century.

2. *Toberacs*, and in the Soule language *Cinzarroxacs* ("noise of little bells"). They are " *Charivaris*," fallen, it is true, into disuse, meant to stigmatize a second marriage, or conjugal infidelity. They are held during the month or months preceding the second marriage, or as long as conjugal infidelity is talked of, and at night, in the neighbourhood of the house of the betrothed, but at a respectful distance. It is there that one or two *Coblacari*, in the most awful din of bells and ox-horns, &c., try the patience of the betrothed by versified dialogues or songs, full of malicious allusions, &c.

3. *Tobero-munstracs, Asto-lurterracs*. They are also a sort of carnival, which only differs from the preceding ones by the solemnity given to it, and by the place where it is held. To say nothing of all the disorders arising from them, the expense of these "charivaris" prevents their taking place very often. When they are held, it is in the public squares, before an enormous gathering of people, col-

lected there from every corner of the Basque country.

4. *Mascarades.* They must not be confounded with those carnivals which sprung from the *Bacchanalia, Saturnalia,* &c., of the Romans. These mascarades, still in honour in Soule, are only pantomimes. . . . They existed in Spain and France ages ago.

5. *Dancing.* If we were to believe a certain Pierre de l'Ancre, a Boileau, a Hamilton, &c., " Basque priests dance, and are the first to go to the country balls. . . . A Basque child knows how to dance before knowing how to call his father and his nurse! . . . Joy begins with life, and only ends at death!!!" &c., &c.

These are indeed historians (not history) bravely quoted by certain authors, because it pleases them to write without knowing what they write about!

What is certain, and proved beyond dispute, is that dancing (always excluding the mingling of sexes, except in the presence of fathers and mothers) formerly existed among the Basques, as an honest amusement and a bodily exercise. But modern dances, which I will call horrible pantomimes, have as yet no name in our language, and are happily unknown in our valleys, still free from the ignominies of modern civilization.

6. *Jeu de paume* (hand-ball). The really and exclusively national game of the Basques is the *jeu de paume*: and there is no village, however poor or isolated, without its *rebot*, where not only young, but middle-aged men, in presence of the whole village, play with a passion only equal to their agility, vigour, and suppleness, those games so disputed and popular. .... These sports sometimes bring together five, ten, and even fifteen thousand Basques from both sides of the Pyrenees, as for instance during the glorious days of the *Gascoïna*, in Spain.

CUSTOMS OF THE BASQUES.

There are a thousand accusations, both foolish and unfair, current against the Basques. .... The Basques are not "superstitious," but "religious," which is not the same thing. .... All the efforts of Jeanne d'Albret, &c., have failed to introduce a single Protestant

notion here... They are civil and kind...
they address you uncovered, and always salute
you (save in towns). They most willingly
leave their fields to guide or direct travellers,
and expect nothing more than a thankful acknowledgment... They are also hospitable...
and in their houses, always wonderfully clean,
they at once give the "place of honour" to a
stranger, in the secular seat called çuçulia,
which has been there for centuries near the
hearth, and will thus pass to all future generations. For the night, they are sure to give
you the best room they possess.....

Whatever may have been the causes which
first induced the Basques to emigrate to America, it is now an established fact, that almost
every Basque family has one or several of its
members on the banks of the Rio de la Plata.
But we cannot shut our eyes to the great
amount of money they send home; to say nothing of those "Americans" who, when they
return, enter, by marriage, into the best houses
of our country, or build those splendid houses
often seen in Labourd, &c.

They form homogeneous populations in many parts of America, especially at Buenos-Ayres, where they now have their own priests, churches, &c.

HARISTOY,
Parish-priest of Sauguis.

CHAPTER V.

THE BASQUES.

THE preceding chapter (IV.), written by a Basque himself, shows the antiquity of this mysterious race; but when and from what land it first came to Europe, is a problem which history alone will perhaps never solve, although numberless volumes have been written about it.* According to Humboldt, the Basques really were the first inhabitants of Spain. Abyssinia, Carthage, South America, India, are some of the countries from which they are supposed to have slowly migrated. Perhaps geology may help to clear this much-agitated question.

The Basques were probably of Iberian or Cantabrian origin, and preceded the Celts by twenty centuries. They were called *Euskarians*, when the Phenicians came, in the year 1100 A.D. Numbers of them are now quite fair, and most of them are tall; so their type appears to have much changed since Tacitus,

* See the work of *Chaho*.

Basque History and Tongue. 53

who described the Iberians as brown men, with frizzled hair. In any case, they differ widely from what Voltaire cynically called them—"*Un petit peuple qui saute et danse au haut des Pyrénées*"!!

The Basques are certainly not less than 3000 years old, and as far as we know they were never conquered. Neither the Celts, Vandals, Romans, nor Moors could make them yield. Later, they resisted and checked the armies of Clovis. They had excellent weapons; their sword was adopted by the Romans, and Horace praised their shields. Lucan says the Pyrenæan Iberians were "the terror of the world." (See *Chaho*.)

Besides history, many of their customs prove their antiquity; and in the Basque language (*Escuara*), which is unhappily fast dying out, Biblical traditions are often quite plain, *viz.* *Semé* means "son" (*Sem*, Noah's son), &c.

The origin of this extremely old and mysterious language is little known, so different is it from all idioms ever heard of. Sanscrit has some analogies with it. Here is a specimen of a Basque word:

Azpilcuetagaraycosaroyarenberecolarrea, which means, "Lower field of the high hill of Azpicuelta." Stuttering is hopeless for a Basque.

There are many idioms or dialects in Basque, as the Spaniards often misunderstand the French. It has been said of the Basques, that they write "Solomon," and pronounce it "Nebuchadnezzar"!!

Wherever they came from, these bold mountaineers certainly are a most manly, adventurous, honest, and handsome race, numbering at present, according to an excellent authority (Francisque Michel), about 840,000 (700,000 in Spain alone). This seems, however, far beyond the number. They love the sea beyond all things, and are first-rate sailors. It is almost beyond dispute that they discovered the coasts of North America. Nomadic and restless, they emigrate in thousands to the Rio de la Plata; but their deep love of their country almost always carries them home again as soon as their fortune is made. There are about 100,000 Basques in South America. Inland, they are eminently a pastoral people.

Their strength, agility, and endurance are proverbial: "To run, to jump like a Basque," is a common saying all over France. They are also very persevering. In fact, they are, with the Bretons, the most manly of all Frenchmen.

It does one good to live with men so cheerful and honest. Very reserved at first, until they know you well, they soon become inquisitive and familiar, but always respectful. As for drunkards, beggars, or thieves, they are almost unknown in this happy country.

Patriarchal, but warlike, the Basques are also an eminently religious people, and deeply Catholic. Their churches (where the sexes are always separated) are both large and handsome, and quite full on Sundays. Very often these buildings have strange steeples with three points, supposed by many authors to represent the Blessed Trinity: this, however, is much disputed. A thousand stentorian voices, singing in unison under those sacred roofs, shake the walls, and prove that the Basques possess strong lungs as well as religious fervour. In fact, there is a sort of wild energy in every action, thought, or impulse of this powerful race, far superior to the lazy Gascons and more or less effeminate Spaniards living around it in the same climate.

A Basque is always active. If he is not labouring in the fields, he will spend hours in his tennis-court, playing the *jeu de paume* with as much energy as if it were a battle-field. Every Basque village has its *jeu de paume*, where the French and Spaniards meet in hundreds or thousands, till one side finds its Waterloo.

Dancing and all athletic sports are in universal esteem; but at dances the sexes are always kept apart, just as at church. Then in autumn the Basques have "pastorals," played in the open air (see Chapter IV.). Accoutred in fanciful costumes, the performers are on horseback. The subjects are taken from Scripture, or from Tasso, Dante, &c. The prophet Jeremiah once appeared with the Crimean medal!!

Though the language is rich and harmonious, the literature is said to be rather meagre.

Amongst the old and strange institutions of this very peculiar race, we must mention the "Assembly of States," called *Bilsar* in times gone by—*Bilsar* meaning strictly "assembly of old men," like the Latin *senatus* (*senum cœtus*).

"It is in woods of ancestral oaks that landowners and heads of families used to meet and settle the administrative rules of all the communes. There, standing with their backs to the ancient trees, leaning on their medlar-tree sticks, they discussed, deliberated in perfect liberty, and they took decisions which more than once compelled the kings of France and of Navarre to yield to their *fueros* (privileges). Two rocks served as a seat for the president and his secretary; whilst another block, roughly polished, was the table upon which were engraved the decisions arrived at.

"The origin of the *bilsar* is lost in obscurity, but it is believed to have preceded the establishment of Christianity among the Basques. What gives a great foundation for this opinion is the fact that priests were excluded from it, though the country was deeply religious; no doubt it was thought objectionable to modify the original constitution which ruled public affairs."—(*Cambo*, &c., by C. Duvoisin.)

Physically, the Basques are tall and muscular, but, above all, supple and swift-footed; they are indefatigable pedestrians. In their eyes there is both energy and haughtiness, though blue eyes are common among them. The women are superb, and have beautiful hair. The Basque type seems a mixed one and we may mention as a very strange fact, which seems to be well authenticated, that as late as the year 1790 specimens of real savages were found in the forest of *Iraty*. Gipsies are numerous.

A curious stick, called *makila*, is used all over the country. Made of the medlar-tree, it is often worth more than a guinea. There are plenty to be had at Bayonne.

Here are a few Basque words, which may be useful in travelling:—

Bread—Oguia.
Wine—Arnoa.
Water—Ura.
Salt—Gatza.
Pepper—Bipherra.
Breakfast—Gosaria.
Dinner—Bazcaria.
Table—Mahaina.
Spoon—Golbarea.
Fork—Sardesca.
Plate—Gathelua.
Knife—Ganibeta.
Glass—Gandola.
Cup—Kikera.
Soup—Elcecoa.
Beef—Idikia.
Mutton—Cikitekia.

Veal—Aratchekia.
Fowl—Oilokia.
Milk—Esnia.
Sugar—Azucrea.
Tea—Dutia.
Butter—Burra.
Cheese—Gasna.
Eggs—Arroltceac.
Potatoes—Lur-Sagarra.
Brandy—Aguardienta.

Pear—Udaria.
Apple—Sagarra.
Cherry—Guerecia.
Grape—Mahatsa.
Orange—Iranya.
Lemon—Citroina.

Basque Words.

Strawberry—Marhubia.
Salmon—Izokina.
Trout—Amarraina.

Chair—Kadera.
Bed—Ohea.
Door—Bortha.
Key—Gakhoa.
Window—Leihoa.
Candle—Gandera.
Inn—Ostatua.
Horse—Zaldia.
Donkey—Astoa.
Dog—Zakhurra.
Rat—Garratoina.

Fire.—Sua.
Firewood—Errekina.

Gold—Urrhea.
Silver—Cilharra.
Copper—Cobrea.

Mountain—Mendia.
Forest—Oihana.
Road—Bidea.
Grotto—Harpia.
Flower—Lorea.
Monday—Astelehena.
Tuesday—Asteartea.
Wednesday—Asteazkena.

Thursday—Ortceguna.
Friday—Ortciralea.
Saturday—Larunbatea.
Sunday—Igandea.
To-day—Egun.
To-morrow—Bihar.
Yesterday—Atzo.
Morning—Goiza.
Evening—Arratsa.
Night—Gaua.
Never—Nibolz.
Always—Bethi.

Rain—Uria.
Snow—Elhurra.

Hot—Bero.
Cold—Hotz.
Pretty—Pullit.
Ugly—Itsusi.
Young—Gazte.
Old—Zahar.

Man—Guizon.
Woman—Emastea.
Boy—Muthicoa.
Girl—Donceila.
Child—Haurra.

Large—Handi.
Small—Ttipi.

EXTRACTS ON THE BASQUES,

Taken from the 'Penny Magazine' (1842).

". . . . The Basque language is generally supposed to be totally different from all the European languages, an assertion from which entire assent may be reasonably withheld for the present. . . . . If we are to believe the Basque grammarians, their language existed before the building of the Tower of Babel, and was brought to Spain by Tubal. Setting aside such extravagances, it may be remarked that the testimonies adduced to prove that the Basque language was spoken by all, or nearly all the primitive inhabitants of the Peninsula, are so numerous and conclusive, as to amount almost to a demonstration. . . . . The number of Basque words existing in the names of places in Italy (of which Orvieto and Urbino may be quoted among others), is perhaps a sufficient proof that some of the inhabitants of both these countries once spoke the same language. . . . . The Basques were the only Spaniards who preserved their independance, not having been subdued by any of the nations who invaded the Peninsula. Pompey was the first who in the year 60 A.D. led the Roman legions into that country; but the passage of Strabo quoted to prove that he built Pamplona, was evidently not intended by the author to signify anything of the kind . . . . no less obstinate was their resistance against the Goths. . . . .

"The government of the (Spanish) Basque provinces differs entirely from that of the rest of the Peninsula. Every province has its own constitution and a separate government, not differing much in spirit and form from each other. The people of Alava, at a very remote epoch, which some historians suppose to have been prior to the invasion of the Arabs, appointed their civil and military governors at a general assembly. This assembly met every year at the Campo de Arnaja (?), a plain near Vitoria. It was composed of the bishop and archdeacon, of all the secular clergy of the province, and all the principal men; including also ladies, who were the representatives of their families. . . . . In the year 1457, at an assembly held at Rivabellosa, by order of Enrique IV. of

Castile, a collection of the laws and privileges of Alava was formed and approved; and by that code they are governed at present. . . . .

"There is no building belonging to the state; and even the prisons belong to private individuals, who let them to the state. The people pay only one direct tax, which consists in a moderate rate for every house, and is equally divided; so that the rich and the poor contribute to the state the same sum. The revenues of the Church are so scanty, that the richest abadia, or rectory, is not worth more than 140*l.* per annum.

"The chief privileges of the Viscayans consist:—

"In paying no taxes except those levied by their Juntas.

"In every Viscayan Hidalgo, or 'gentleman,' (and acknowledged as such in every part of Spain) not being subject to any tribunal, or to any other laws (either in their own province or in any other part of the Peninsula) than their own, and in having a judge resident in Valladolid for the administration of those laws in cases occurring out of the province.

"In being exempt from military service, except in the defence of their own country.

"In the enjoyment of commercial liberty; and finally, in not having any officers appointed by the government of Madrid, except the masters of the Post-office.

"The Basques of the three provinces (Spanish) also contribute to the royal exchequer a certain 'voluntary donation.' . . .

"The Viscayans and Guipuzcoans are the best sailors in the Peninsula, and skilful in commercial transactions. They are very active and industrious. Their chief occupations are agriculture, commerce, and the manufacturing of iron. The women assist the men in the cultivation of the ground, and are remarkable for their cleanliness. Their manners are simple and easy; they are fond of dancing at their festivities, and enjoying the moderate pleasures of the table.

"Their national instruments are the tambourine and the bagpipe. Their dance is quick and lively, and is always accompanied by singing. In their weddings they greet the bride in going to and coming from church, by firing guns and pistols, and very often she is induced to fire them herself.

"In some villages, after the burial ceremony is over, they distribute bread, cheese, wine, and walnuts among the persons invited; and some beg money to pay for masses for the release of the souls of the deceased from purgatory.

"The dress of the men and women is similar to that of the mountaineers of Castile: both wear a species of shoe which is made of a hard and untanned piece of hog-skin, or that of any other animal, which they soften by soaking it in water, and then cut it into pieces of the size of the foot, which they fasten on by strings.

"The Basques are in general frugal, cheerful, honest, and courteous, without meanness. When kindly treated, they are docile and manageable, but if they are dealt with severely and harshly, they become stubborn and intractable, and it is for that reason that they are with great difficulty subjected to severe military discipline, particularly by officers who are not of their own country. Gonzalve de Cordova, from the experience he had of them in Sicily, often said that he would rather keep lions than Viscayans. They are a brave people, and better adapted for a system of guerilla warfare than any other nation in Spain."

CONCLUSIONS OF THE REV. W. WEBSTER, UPON THE BASQUES.

(See *Société Ramond's* Bulletin of April, 1872.)

"These points we think may be regarded as more or less definitely established:—

"(1.) That the Basque or Escualdun race, a people of many tribes, was very early settled in Spain, in the south of France, in Corsica, and in Sicily.

"(2.) That they are the race more or less vaguely designated by the Greeks as Iberians.

"(3.) That Celtic races immediately succeeded them, overlaid, and to a certain extent mingled with them, as the Celtiberi, &c., of classical authors.

"(4.) That the Basques were established in their present position in France long anterior to the sixth century, A.D.

"(5.) That the Basque language (Escuara) belongs to the Turanian family of languages; either to the Finnic branch, or to the North-American Indian.

"(6.) That the Basques, instead of being a darker, are, on the whole, a fairer people than any of their neighbours.

"(7.) To these may perhaps be added, that the form of the Basque skull is peculiar. . . .

"Wherein lies the interest of this question: Who are the Basques? In this, that it is, in some sort, a crucial problem for philology and ethnology. Philology declares the Basques to be a Turanian race. Their present physical features, excepting the alleged small capacity of the cerebrum, present one of the finest types of the Indo-Caucasian race.

"The problems to be solved are these: Have the Basques, by the influence of climate or civilization, changed in physical features from a Turanian to an Aryan type? or have they, originally an Aryan race, in some way acquired a Turanian language? Or, have all Aryan races gone successively through a monosyllabic, agglutinative, and inflexional form of language; but the Basques stopped short, like the Turanian races, at the agglutinative stage? Or, has the change in their physique been simply the effect of intermixture with Aryan, Semitic, and especially Celtic blood?

"Can these questions be satisfactorily answered? We think not, at present. . . . . Are they likely to be so in future? Or is the problem insoluble? We answer hopefully; but we think the solution is to be sought rather from Anthropology and pre-historic Archæology than from any fresh light to be drawn from historic records. To us it seems that in the Basques we have, as it were, an older stratum of our race, one once widely spread, now only cropping up through the posterior and overlying strata in one corner of the Western Pyrenees, and probably somewhat metamorphosed in its passage through the incumbent and neighbouring strata; but we have some slight indications in the classical authors of its presence on the surface in older times, in other localities. We believe that it is still possible for the three youthful sciences of comparative Philology, pre-historic Archæology, and Ethnology, to determine with more or less exactitude the place of the Escualdun in the history of mankind, and no slight aid towards this result we think will be given by the work which we have just reviewed."*

* (*Note au sujet de l'ouvrage de M. Bladé sur l'origine des Basques, par* M. W. WEBSTER.)

CHAPTER VI.

BASQUE COUNTRY.

THOUGH its boundaries are very vague, at least in Spain, the Basque territory is much larger than is generally supposed. In Spain it consists of *Navarre, Guipuzcoa, Alava, Biscaye,* and part of *Asturias,* and contains, according to Francisque Michel, about 700,000 inhabitants. In France it is nothing like so large, and much less populous (140,000 inhabitants. See Chap. V.). But its limits are better defined; you always know when you pass them. It is composed of *Soule, Labourd,* and *Basse-Navarre.* (See map.) Altogether, the Basque country, including French and Spanish provinces, is about as large as Wales.

The land is very green, undulating, and picturesque, some of the hills being upwards of 6000 feet high; and if you reach any height, no matter where, you are certain to get an extensive and varied view of mountains and plains, and often of the sea, besides streams and beautiful rivers, such as the Nive, Adour, Bidassoa, Bidouze, &c., which irrigate green plains as rich as any in England. If you stand on the plains, far from the Pyrenees, at Biarritz for instance, you get an immense view of mountains, forming a long, jagged line of 150 miles. Then there are countless villages, with their handsome churches and walls of dazzling whiteness, with strange blood-red lines on them. The Basque architecture is very peculiar. Now and then you come to old manors covered with ivy, and belonging to what are called "Americans," the name given to wealthy Basques who have made their fortune in South America.

Basque villages are not compact and regular; they are rather a disorderly accumulation of houses scattered upon a very large surface, without forming streets. The inns are always clean, very cheap, and well supplied; but French is seldom understood. Wood, in some parts, is fifteen times cheaper than at Pau or Bayonne.

On the whole, the Basque coasts are wild and barren, very like Connemara or Donegal; but on the hills inland you will find the largest forests in the Pyrenees; you can travel 30 miles in some of them (*Iraty*, for instance), and have very good sport; there are bears, wild boars, wolves, and izards; quails, figpeckers, partridges, thrushes, eagles, bustards, and wild ducks, &c., &c., besides the *palombes*, or ring-doves, wonderfully fast birds, which come in thousands in the autumn, and are caught in huge nets, as they attempt to cross the Pyrenees.

The wild singing swan has been seen, but seldom, during extremely cold winters.

There is trout in all the streams, and salmon is common in the Bidassoa, the Nive, &c.

There is nothing in France more beautiful than the Basque Pyrenees; and the only unpleasant thing to be said against them is the changeableness of the weather, a misfortune common and peculiar to most countries placed between mountains and the sea. The climate is maritime, wet and boisterous. It is more than redeemed, however, by the scenery, the exquisite verdure of the foliage and fields, and the graceful undulations of the soil, which give the whole country the rich but pastoral aspect of a great English park. Only lakes are wanting. Some peaks (those above 5000 feet) are very bleak indeed, and snow-capped for six months in the year; but even there vegetation and cottages are still found at very great heights.

It is a populous country, although there are no large towns. Houses are always in sight. There is no Basque village without at least one very neat little inn, where you are sure to get good beds, mutton, fowls, and eggs, besides game in the season, and at very low prices — an excellent dinner coming to a shilling! In fact, with five francs a day, pedestrians can cross the Basque country in every direction. It is perhaps the cheapest place in all Europe. With 10*l.* to spare, a good walker could easily explore it all in about three weeks. The average distance between two villages is about 20 miles. So you need not take provisions. All you want is a map (*État-major*), a compass, and a stick. You can send on any luggage you may want by the diligences, which cross every road in the country; but a knapsack is indispensable in the wild regions touching the Pyrenees.

Autumn is by far the best season for travelling, being mild and clear.

The roads are excellent; there is such a network of them, that a carriage can reach almost any locality, on both sides of the Basque Pyrenees; but if you want to cross the chain from France to Spain, you can only drive over in two places, along the coast, or from Bayonne to Pampeluna, by the *Maya* col, east of La Rhune. However, in a few years a road for carriages will probably ascend the Col de *Roncevaux*.

These fine hills are best suited to good pedestrians, who, without being enthusiastic mountaineers, disdain monotonous walking on straight or level roads. But, strange to say, a good guide is in these Pyrenees almost indispensable, perhaps more so than in the loftier and snowy parts of the main chain, where you can so often at one glance, by standing on an isolated summit, survey in the morning all the details of the country stretching like a map under your feet, study an entire province before exploring it, and make your way accordingly. In this intricate mountain region, where very few summits rise to any great height above their immediate neighbours, you can more easily get lost than in the Alps, because you seldom see very far before you, and your horizon is both confused and limited. Then the Basque hills are grouped with great irregularity, so that the countless little valleys which descend towards the plains seldom go straight for more than two or three miles, but wind their way down capriciously like long snakes. They are as tortuous and numerous as veins in the human body; in fact, you never steer for more than half an hour in the same direction. Besides this, there are immense forests, where if once lost in a mist, you might wander hopelessly for a week; and dreadfully narrow gorges with banks running down, at unpleasant angles, into furious torrents. A good guide is therefore advisable.

Better have a passport, which may be sometimes asked for near the Spanish frontier.

Always make friends with "gendarmes" and "douaniers"; for they might become unpleasant enemies.

As for "diligences," the reader can take it for granted that one or two are sure to run daily between all the towns mentioned, if a road connects them. Prices are very low.

CHAPTER VII.

CAMBO.

FEW people spend a day at Biarritz without visiting the pretty Basque town of Cambo, and the *Pas de Roland*, close to it. There is a carriage-road to both; and a rather dislocated kind of vehicle, pompously called a "diligence," goes daily from Bayonne to Cambo, starting from the southern end of the town (*Porte d'Espagne*).

Cambo lies to the south-east of Biarritz, just at the foot of the Pyrenees; and you have the choice of three roads, all good for carriages :—

From Biarritz to Cambo by Anglet, 15 miles.

From Biarritz to Cambo by the Négresse railway station, also 15 miles.

From Biarritz to Cambo by Bayonne, 19 miles.

Most people go by Anglet, as the road is better than by the Négresse. You take the Bayonne road as far as the fifth kilomètre (three miles), where you turn to the right, on a rather bad road for two miles, until you cross the railway to Madrid, and enter the Bayonne and Pampeluna first-class road, at two miles and a half from the former. You then go due south, through an undulating and picturesque country, where little woods alternate with great moors, and with the blue and intricate line of the Basque Pyrenees before you. You hear the Atlantic roaring behind you.

After leaving on your right a conical and wooded hill (*Ste. Barbe*), worth climbing for the view's sake, you suddenly find yourself on a high elevation, with the lovely basin of *Ustaritz* and the winding *Nive* under your feet. You then descend to this important Basque village (11 miles from Biarritz), whose walls are as white as Carrara marble, and glitter gaily in the sun. It is fully a mile long, and has a handsome church (Gothic). All the shutters are green or red; everything looks neat, comfortable, and gay; in fact, you guess at once you have entered the Basque country. Population, 2327 inhabitants.

There are many "Americans" at Ustaritz,

that is, as we have before said, Basque colonists who have made a fortune on the Rio de la Plata, and then come home. Here and there you see mills and manufactories. Salmon is abundant in the river.

It was at Ustaritz that the last Viscounts of Lapurdunum (Bayonne) ended their days; and it is in a grove of most venerable old oaks close by that the "general assemblies" of old men (in Basque *bilzar*) used to meet. The president and his secretary alone sat on a rock, whilst the members each stood gravely against a tree. (See Germond de Lavigne's '*Biarritz*,' &c.)

At a mile beyond Ustaritz, you leave on the right the road to *Pampeluna* (53 miles from here; and a few minutes after you pass under the walls of an imposing building (right), the *Laressore* seminary.

Then you soon come to the last hill before Cambo, and ascend it by a most gentle and graceful curve. (Here, if on foot, you can take a short cut to the left, and save half a mile.) Look back at the charming and green valley of the winding Nive, with the snow-white walls of Ustaritz smiling on its banks, and here and there a light bridge joining them. On your left, far below, you see the foam of the "rapids," called *Nasses*. The whole scene is like a great park, with blue Scotch hills, and the sky of Italy.

At last you reach *Upper* Cambo, and another mile takes you down to the *Lower* or *Bas-Cambo*, where you find a good hotel, close to the Nive (*Saint Martin*). You are here 14 miles from Bayonne and 15 from Biarritz (by the way you came).

The *Négresse* road is rather bad in some places for carriages. You go to the railway station, cross the line, and then ascend a little hill beyond; after which, leaving on your right the *Arcangues* and *St. Pée* road, you travel east, parallel to the Madrid and Bayonne railway, which runs on your left. At three miles from the Négresse (five from Biarritz), you meet the Bayonne and Pampeluna road, at three miles from the former and ten from Cambo. After this you go on as above.

If you go to Cambo from Biarritz, by way of Bayonne, the distance is 19 miles, and you then have the choice of both banks of the Nive. If you take the *left* bank, you leave

Bayonne by the *Porte d'Espagne* (south) and the churchyard, and soon pass (one mile) the ruins of *Marrac*, sold to Napoleon in 1808, and burnt in 1825. At Marrac Napoleon obliged Ferdinand VII. to abdicate.

Three miles from Bayonne take you to the junction of this and the preceding road, where you enter the Basque country. But if you take the *right* bank of the Nive, you must start from Bayonne by *Mousserolles*, its south-eastern suburb (left bank of the Adour). Crossing the Pau railway, you soon go through *St. Pierre d'Irube* and several fine estates, after which, leaving on your left the main road, which goes to Oloron, take a narrower one, and go south. Passing the great salt-works (three miles) of *Villefranque*, then the village of the same name, you will reach *Ustaritz* in about the same time as by the left bank of the Nive. (From Ustaritz, see above.)

Cambo is a village of about 1500 inhabitants, covering much extent on both banks of the beautiful *Nive*, perhaps the clearest stream of all the Pyrenees, and here a noisy torrent, as wild as a youth just escaping from school.

Even after leaving its mountains, and entering a comparatively level country, it is almost as restless as ever, and is only rendered navigable by the help of man. Wherever the river is shallow and wide, part of its bed has been artificially contracted into a narrow space, only two or three feet wide, where the waters rush furiously, like "rapids" in miniature, through a kind of corridor, between two walls of palisades. These rapids are called *Nasses*, and through them boats shoot down quite safely like arrows. Accidents *do* happen, but seldom. The *Nasses* can even be ascended: but it thus takes seven hours from Bayonne to Cambo, and only two to go down! (distance by water, about 16 miles). It is, however, an expensive journey, costing at the least 20 francs.

The word "Cambo" comes either from "Campus," or from the Celtic *Cam* ("a curve").

There are remains of an important camp called, as usual, "Cæsar's," at a mile S.S.E. of the town. Its Roman origin is very doubtful; still, it bears the traces of a very clever system of defence, and 20,000 men could have entrenched themselves in it.

The Pyrenees begin just behind Cambo,

and make it a lovely place, but they are very low, the highest point being under 3000 feet. The charm of this popular spot chiefly consists in its verdure, its woods, its peace and seclusion from every noise of the world, and its calm and mild atmosphere, scarcely ever disturbed by the gentlest breeze. It looks like a nest under a mountain. The leaves are quite green till November, and though no wind can ever blow strongly in such a sheltered place, the influence of the hot south wind and its fiery blasts often makes it almost too warm in midwinter; because, before reaching the Basque country, it does not sweep over snowy deserts and cool itself, as it must do at Pau, and most places north of the Pyrenees.

The bathing season (sulphurous and ferruginous baths) lasts till November.

(The bathing establishment is in Lower Cambo, quite near the Hotel St. Martin.)

You should not fail to go and see the view from the churchyard (Upper Cambo). The post-office is in Upper Cambo, and some hotels, at a height of 200 feet above the sea-level. Very good chocolate.

Salmon is abundant in the river, trout also;

and the fishing season lasts from the 1st of February until the end of October.

The waters of the Nive often rise in spring or in autumn, fifteen or twenty feet, and the floods are fearful. See the mark of the highest level reached, on the wall of the bathing establishment (June, 1856).

Out of the season Cambo contains nothing but Basques; but in summer, it is full of strangers, and amongst its illustrious visitors, we must mention the two Napoleons.

The shade and the verdure almost everywhere found both in and around this charming place, make it doubly pleasant after Biarritz. But it is a pity that you cannot, even on foot, (except by scrambling) ascend the banks of the river, to the *Pas de Roland*. You can only follow them up for a little distance. Turning your back to the hotel, and taking the left bank, you walk for a little while on a tolerable footpath, well sheltered from the sun, and through immense ferns, with here and there a tall foxglove, but the track comes to an end after a short mile. If you wish to go on, you must here leave the Nive, and ascending a few minutes to the right, you soon find two houses, near one of which (that on the left) the track continues west, with a good view to the south. Now the road gradually turns northward, and takes you back, after a steep descent through stones and ferns, to your starting-point. It is a walk of about two miles and a half, and perhaps the best thing you could do at Cambo, if you have only an hour or less to spare.

But if you have time, you should certainly go to the PAS DE ROLAND. It is a tall and wild rock, with a great hole running right through it, on the left bank of the green and deep Nive, whose waters perhaps once crossed this strange orifice or made it; but an absurd and popular legend attributes it to the famous Roland, the paladin of old, who kicked the rock, and with his boot or sword thus opened a passage for himself.

You can now drive to the Pas de Roland. Leaving Upper Cambo on an excellent road, and going due south, through a hilly country full of pretty villas and cherry-trees, you come to the village of *Itsatsou* (two miles and a half), with a very rich church. You then enter a sad and rugged gorge, with, however, some splendid chestnut-trees, which soon cease; mountain scenery here begins in earnest. The Nive is on your left, and its emerald-green waters are transparent as glass; you can almost count the rocks forming black spots at the bottom, at depths of twelve and fifteen feet. Four miles from Cambo, you reach the *Pas de Roland*.

The carriage-road stops here; but you can walk along the Nive to *Bidarraÿ* (six miles, see Chap. XVI.), and so follow it up to its very sources (37 miles from here. See Chap. XVI.).

Cambo to *Hasparren*, seven miles; to *St. Jean Pied de Port*, 25 miles. (You drive both.)

With half a day to spare, travellers to Cambo may ascend (on horseback or on foot) the easy *Pic de Mondarrain*, only seven miles distant, and rising 2460 feet, nearly due south of Cambo. It is a conical and bare but very *popular* mountain, seen from almost everywhere in the Biarritz country, and unmistakable.

You go to *Itsatsou* (see above), and then begin to rise, at first under the shade of oaks and cherry-trees, but very soon in a great wilderness of ferns, passing near a ferruginous spring. Two hours and a half from Cambo, will place you on the top, where the view is splendid, combining a vast extent of sea and plains, with mountains. On this windy summit, are ponderous ruins of what must once have been (thirteenth century) an imposing and useful fort, the walls being five feet thick. Battles, in fact, were probably fought there, and a passage south of it is called "the defile of bones," a sinister and significative appellation! The rocks are quartz, limestone, and clay-slate.

In 1813, the French had a battery there.

By going down a little more westward than the preceding route, and following a stream, you can reach *Espelette* (Hotel du Mondarrain), whence to Cambo, three miles.

Espelette is a large village of 1500 inhabitants, on the first-class international road from Bayonne to Pampeluna, only 14 miles from the former. It is a wealthy place, and in a most charming country. See the church and *château*, once belonging to the Counts of Espeleta, a very old family, finally settled in Spain.

CHAPTER VIII.

ST. JEAN DE LUZ.

ST. JEAN DE LUZ is on the Bayonne and Madrid Railway, and eight miles from the Biarritz *station*, but ten from the *town*. All trains stop there.

It is a strange and melancholy, but picturesque town, of now 3000 inhabitants, or even less, though it once had four times that number. Now fallen and silent, it is all full of glorious " souvenirs." It existed in the sixth century; *Lohitzun*, its Basque name, meaning "a marsh."

Hotels:—*De la Poste* (on the right as you enter by the road); *de France* (near the church); &c.

It is very well paved, well built, and clean; but its chief attractions are the country surrounding it, the mountain of *La Rhune* (see Chap. XIII.), in fact, the scenery and walks. For half an hour is enough to dispose of the church, where Louis XIV. married, of his house, and that of the young Infanta he chose for his wife (1660).

A good pedestrian will prefer walking back to Biarritz (10 miles), and must even do so, or drive home, unless he waits for the late evening train to Bayonne. He can save a mile by taking a bye-road which turns to the left on the top of the hill of *Bidart*, a village four miles from Biarritz, and where you leave the Basque country. But on the western side of the Bois de Boulogne and its lake (see Chap. III.), there is a treacherous morass or bog, with pools beneath, not very safe when it gets dark.

You can also walk from Biarritz to St. Jean de Luz by the sea-side; but it is thus 15 miles instead of 10, and after *Guétharry*, unsafe for a lady. The four first miles of sand to Bidart are only fatiguing; but there you meet a first obstacle in the shape of a little river, to cross which you must lose ten minutes, the bridge being inland. Then, beyond *Guétharry* (two hotels, five miles from Biarritz), the coast becomes alternately very precipitous and cut up into bays, where you have to double the distance (even before high water), and make weary semicircles in yielding sand. In fact, it is better, and far shorter, once you pass Guétharry, to ascend and follow the summit of the cliffs; but even by this route you can seldom go straight.

The HISTORY of St. Jean de Luz is too interesting to be wholly omitted.

After bravely resisting and checking the Normans in the ninth century, it had already become a flourishing town in the thirteenth century, when whale-fishing was in its palmy days.

Its proud inhabitants then enjoyed wonderful liberties, and their immunities were confirmed by Louis XI., who spent a long time there in 1463.

A pilot of St. Jean de Luz (Sanchez de Huelva) is said to have first suggested to Columbus the possible existence of America. In any case, its sailors knew Iceland very well as far back as 1412, and there is little doubt about their having discovered Newfoundland in the middle of the fifteenth century, many years before the great discovery of Columbus.

Francis I. spent a few hours here after his captivity.

The town was taken and burnt by the

Spaniards in 1558, and a few years after (1565) it was visited by Charles IX. It was towards the close of the same century that 500 persons were cruelly burnt to death for sorcery. About the same period, whales gradually disappeared from the Bay of Biscay, going to northern oceans,—a severe loss for the almost exclusively "maritime" population of these regions. Still, the manly sailors of St. Jean de Luz, far from losing courage, pursued the "monsters of the deep" as far as the Spitzbergen seas, and also went to Newfoundland for cod-fishing, in 200 and 300-ton ships. How times have changed! How empty and silent its roadstead and long streets now seem!

This doomed and unhappy town was retaken by the Spaniards in 1636, and the *Socoa* fort was built in 1640, although the present pier only dates from 1829.

But the greatest, or at least the most memorable event connected with the history of St. Jean de Luz, was the marriage of Louis XIV. (June, 1660) with the Infanta of Spain, Maria-Theresa, of Austria. The great monarch spent six weeks in the town.

Then dawned the most prosperous days of

this now melancholy place. Under Colbert (end of seventeenth century), it had eighty first-class vessels, manned by 3000 magnificent sailors. But hundreds of its brave children fell at the naval disaster of La Hogue (1692).

With the wars of Louis XIV. began its ruin, and it never ceased to decline since. Misery and emigration first contributed to its depopulation, calamities sadly aggravated since that time by the resistless fury and invasion of the ocean, whose first serious advance took place in 1675. It was still worse during the eighteenth century, when the havoc became incredible. Nothing could stand such waves, and the 22nd of January, 1749, was a memorable and fearful day, seven houses being utterly destroyed, and 180 others undermined, and abandoned in a few hours. In 1782 another hurricane swept away all the works of defence and two entire streets, besides a convent of Ursulines, a part of the town being quite submerged by the waves. It was then that Louis XVI., to save St. Jean de Luz from total destruction, began the granite pier of *Ste. Barbe,* on the eastern side of the bay. In three years nearly 500 feet of it had been constructed, and the works resisted the waves for half a century, but at last they also were shattered to pieces, and the great breakwater, now daily and majestically advancing on from the *Socoa* fort eastward, is the only hope left for St. Jean de Luz, where the sea is now encroaching on the land at the rate of a yard per annum, and threatening a dozen houses. In fact, at very low water, heaps of ruins are disclosed on the beach.

Napoleon I. visited St. Jean de Luz in 1808, with gigantic ideas, which all came to nothing, as politics gave him too much trouble, and left him no time to battle with nature. It was in 1819 that the most serious attempts were made to protect this town from its relentless foe, the sea. A kind of " Chinese wall," no less than 50 feet wide, and 33 feet high, with three ranges of huge piles running between it and the sea, was raised like a regular fortification along the side of St. Jean de Luz facing the Atlantic. It was quite Cyclopean, and looked invulnerable; but it was so completely destroyed in 1822 by a hurricane, which lasted a whole week, that according to the report of the engineers themselves, not a fragment of it could be found after! 500 feet of the most formidable masonry were carried off like dust or feathers!

But happily, within the last few years, this fearful sea appears to be relatively calming down, and such paroxysms as those have not been known for fifty years. Besides, the Socoa breakwater is now steadily progressing; it is to be about 1100 feet long, and another is soon to be begun from the other or eastern side of the harbour, where the hill of *Ste. Barbe* projects its mournful ruins against the blue sky. These ruins (a short mile north of St. Jean de Luz) are those of a fort. The view of the Bay of Biscay from this point is superb. It is the same from Socoa, a village and fort standing on the other side, west of St. Jean de Luz (a mile and a half). You can drive to Socoa, and you should not omit to walk a little way to the left (west) of it, where the foam slides up and down the brilliant slopes of schist peculiar to this coast. On sunny days it is a beautiful sight.

To go to Socoa, you first cross the *Nivelle*, a small but pretty stream, which descends from the east of *La Rhune*, through a hilly and very green country: then you enter *Ciboure*, a suburb of St. Jean de Luz, with a large population of gipsies (*cascarotacs*), and a bathing establishment. The men are almost all sailors.

To drive to Socoa, you must now go a very long way round; the direct road along the sea being cut and out of repair. It is a shorter distance to walk than to drive.

The three things to be seen *in* St. Jean de Luz are: the *Church*, built by the English in the thirteenth or fourteenth century. It is in the main street. The *château* where the king spent six weeks, and that of his bride, the Infanta.

There is a good bathing establishment on the northern beach (half a mile), with a *buffet* and reading-room; but it is closed in November.

About 1500 strangers visit the place every summer, and Napoleon III. often came.

The natives are particularly peaceful and friendly, and they always were so: the most perfect security did not cease to exist even in the sanguinary times of the "Terreur." There were only two executions.

N.B.—There are fine fossils on the hill of Ste. Barbe (north side: *Fucoides*).

N.B.—The express train from Paris to Madrid, the one almost always taken to go to St. Jean de Luz, passes through the Biarritz station a little before one o'clock P.M. But no train returns till late in the evening.

CHAPTER IX.

HENDAYE, FUENTERRABIA, SAN SEBASTIAN.

IT is very easy to see these three places in one day from Biarritz, by taking the Paris and Madrid express train at one o'clock P.M. at the Biarritz station (two miles off), and returning by the evening train, which leaves San Sebastian between six and seven o'clock P.M., reaching Biarritz before ten o'clock P.M. By doing it thus you have an hour to spare at the *Irun* station (in Spain), which allows time enough to see *Fuenterrabia* (two miles from the Irun station) and return, so as to continue your journey in the Madrid express, leaving Irun at 2.30 (Spanish time). When you come back in the evening, the train stops another hour at *Hendaye* (towards eight o'clock P.M.), and there you can dine at the railway "table d'hôte."

But some people, to be more free of their motions, prefer driving the whole distance to San Sebastian and back, in all nearly 80

English miles. It is therefore impossible to do it thus on the same day, except with a change of horses at Irun or Hendaye. The only advantage of driving is to leave you ample time for visiting the strange, but very small town of Fuenterrabia, which, let it be remembered, is *not* on the railway, but two miles exactly north of it. The railway route will first be described.

As far as St. Jean de Luz, see preceding chapter. You now travel west, through a hilly country, with deep cuttings, which shut out the view. You can just catch a glimpse (south) of the *Urrugne* village and fields (see below), with the wild mountain of *La Rhune* behind (2920 feet); and beyond (six miles from St. Jean de Luz) you get a passing sight, on your right, of the proud Gothic castle belonging to the great African explorer and *savant*, M. Antoine d'Abbadie. But there is no landscape to speak of till you enter the valley of the *Bidassoa*, after passing a long tunnel, and descend to *Hendaye*, the last station in France (16 miles from the Biarritz station).

It is on the right bank of the *Bidassoa*, and nearly due east of the Spanish town of *Fuen-*

terrabia, well seen on the other side, as the river, although not two miles from its mouth in the ocean, is but two-thirds of a mile across. At all tides, and with the most perfect security, you can go by boat from Hendaye to Fuenterrabia in the smoothest water, the awful surf beyond being quite broken by sandbanks, which look like fragments of a desert. Indeed, this is perhaps the shortest and the best of all ways to see Fuenterrabia without interrupting your journey to San Sebastian. But you would thus have to walk two miles from Fuenterrabia to the station of Irun, where your train stops an hour. It is only a few pence for crossing the *Bidassoa*, a poor but picturesque little river, which flows entirely through Spain for about 30 miles, nearly due north, and then for the last eight miles of its course divides it from France.

Hendaye is only a village of about 700 inhabitants, with a tolerable hotel (*International*), facing the Spanish hill of *Jaysquivel* (2200 feet), so well seen from Biarritz. In 1793 it was mercilessly bombarded at night by the Spaniards of Fuenterrabia, and without any warning. It was reduced to ashes, but fifteen months after the latter town capitulated to 300 French soldiers.

Its liqueur is famous, and the "buffet" at the station not bad.

The scenery is indeed beautiful, though never grand: for wherever you look you see verdure or blue waters, backed by bold brown hills, the highest and most conspicuous of which is the *Haya* (3100 feet), called *Trois-Couronnes* in France, here close by, to the south. Then every acre of the lowlands is dotted with Basque farm-houses, of dazzling whiteness. The sea appears in the distance, as blue as indigo, beyond the waving fields of maize.

The château of M. d'Abbadie, one of the finest in the south of France, and often called *Aragorria*, crowns a hill to the north-east of Hendaye, and three miles from it. The best way up to it is by the beach. After twelve years of travelling in the Ethiopian deserts, this eminent astronomer and linguist has now settled here, on a glorious Basque hill, between the Atlantic and the sky, devoting his life to his wife and science.

After passing Hendaye, the railway to

Madrid crosses the Bidassoa on a handsome bridge, and enters the Spanish province of *Guipuscoa*. On your left (south), high up on a rugged and brown hill, see the white chapel of *St. Martial*, where Marshal Soult, in 1813, unsuccessfully attacked the Spanish troops. (Pilgrimages every year.)*

You now reach *Irun*, the first Spanish town, 18 miles from the Biarritz station, and lying at the foot of the serrated mountain of *Haya* (*Trois-Couronnes*), which rises in gentle slopes south of it (3100 feet), at a distance of three miles as the crow flies, but in reality of about five. Looked at from here, it has a great analogy of shape and of structure with the peak of *La Rhune*, seen from St. Jean de Luz; and its ascent is very much like the one of its neighbour and rival. In other words, it is by the north it is most easily climbed, its western sides being rather precipitous. By the north it is quite easy, and guides are useless. Going at first south from Irun, you soon turn a little to the left, and ascend the first spurs of the mountain, on a reddish soil dotted with chest-

* Since this was written, the Carlists have added a new celebrity to St. Martial.

nut-trees. Then crossing a ravine and a stream, and ascending to the right up a track in zigzags, you reach a bare plateau (just as on La Rhune), north of the ridge, very like a saw, which forms the top. An hour from here, steering south up easy slopes, takes you to the summit (two hours and a half from Irun). It is a long, narrow, and serrated arête, with a marvellous view of sea and mountains, and a great precipice to the west. You see much less of France but more of Spain than from La Rhune, which is also 200 feet lower. Seen from Biarritz, the *Haya* bears S.S.W.

This mountain, where foxes are common, is pierced with galleries and wells for the extraction of iron. Now all abandoned.

A good pedestrian, in a long summer day, can easily ascend the *Trois-Couronnes* from Biarritz, even by taking the one o'clock P.M. train, which will leave him five hours to dispose of at Irun. Driving from Biarritz makes it easier still.

At the Irun station you will always find omnibuses ready to take you either to the town itself (half a mile distant), or to Fuenterrabia. You have an hour to spare.

Here the railway time changes, Madrid time, of course, being adopted. It is twenty-five minutes behind Paris time, and this leaves you an hour's stoppage. No passports required.

You must change trains, as the fears of a French invasion have induced the Spaniards to adopt on their railway lines a gauge wider by a foot than that of their jealous and quarrelsome neighbours.

Besides a *buffet*, there is a large hotel (*de la Viscayna*) near the Irun station, and another in the town (*Arrupe*). The latter is well known to most British tourists.

Irun (in Basque " good place ") has a population of nearly 6000 souls, and a rather heavy-looking, but fine church. Roman walls and medals were found in the neighbourhood.

To see *Fuenterrabia* (two miles north) hire an omnibus or a carriage at the Irun station. The hour you have to spare is quite sufficient. Splendid Indian-corn.

Fuenterrabia (in Basque *Ondarrabia*, "sandy river") is a most thoroughly Spanish town of 3000 inhabitants, with picturesque, but gloomy streets, a crowd of beggars, latticed windows, clouds of dust, and ruined battlements. Desolation is upon it everywhere. Silent and heavy, but pompous *palacios*, with monstrous escutcheons, still bear witness to its ancient splendour. See the church (Gothic inside) and the view from the terrace. See also the *castle*, built towards 907. The Basques are here strikingly handsome.

Battles without end have been fought here, and some walls are riddled with bullets. In 1638, a mutiny having broken out in the French army which besieged it, the garrison made a furious sortie, which cost the French more than 2000 men, mostly drowned in the Bidassoa. In the present century, Fuenterrabia was four times taken and re-taken (1808-1837).

From the light-house of Cape *Figuier* (two miles north of Fuenterrabia), 320 feet above the sea, you can see all the Bay of Biscay; and of course better still, if you ascend the lofty hill of *Jaysquivel*, a bare and breezy ridge, eight miles long, which extends towards the West as far as *Passages* (see below), rising in one place to 2200 feet out of the great Atlantic. If you do this, you will pass by the storm-beaten convent and church of *N. D. de Guadalupe*, so well seen on the hill west of

Fuenterrabia. It is fully three hours' walk over the ridge of Jaysquivel to Passages, and it is both pleasanter and safer always to follow the summit, as the slopes towards the sea are torn all the way by endless and countless ravines, which double the distance.

After this digression, we shall now resume our journey to San Sebastian.

Beyond Irun the line travels west, through a very pretty and fertile country, with bleak hills rising on either side. You soon leave *Renteria* on your left (seven miles from Irun), and then, on your right, the beautiful and almost land-locked little port of *Pasajes*, with bold headlands frowning at its mouth. Here Lafayette sailed for America.

Fantastical villas of every style, scattered everywhere, now give you signs of wealth and civilization as you approach

San Sebastian, a modern and geometrical city of 16,000 inhabitants (17 miles from Irun, 37 from Biarritz). It is the capital of the Basque province of Guipuzcoa.

Omnibuses at the station, which is half a mile from the town. You pass a splendid bridge.

Hotels: *de Inglaterra* (*Beraza*), *de Londres*, *Royal Hôtel*, &c., &c.

The general aspect is rather Parisian than Spanish; the streets are very clean and straight. The town stands on a peninsula, on the south-eastern side of a massive and strongly-fortified hill (*Orgullo*); it is one of the most frequented sea-bathing places in Spain.

See the church of Santa Maria, five minutes' walk from the hotels.

Very good shops, and excellent cigars at *de la Houssaye's, Calle de la Alameda*, 27. You can take back to France, free of duty, as many as will fill your pockets. If it rains, take shelter in the fine *Café de la Marina*, on the *Alameda*, where the garrison band plays on summer evenings, before a procession of lovely Basque women.

But on a fine day you should walk up the hill of *Orgullo*, whose citadel seems to threaten the Atlantic from a height of 375 feet. The view is grand, though the Biarritz coast is hidden by a bold headland. You can ascend the hill on either side, and walk all round it, observing, as you pass its western side, the dilapidated graves of many a British officer. Assaulted and taken in 1813 by the Duke of Wellington, San Sebastian was sacked, and then set on fire. "Facts," says Henry O'Shea in his remarkable *Guide to Spain*, "must not be disfigured to please patriotism, and this is one of the very few black spots on the glorious sun of England." . . . The British loss in this assault amounted to 5000 killed and wounded.

San Sebastian has bull-fights, a theatre, a casino, and there is much gambling.

With a few hours to spend there, you should hire a boat, cross the harbour from east to west, and ascend the pyramidal hill which rises west of San Sebastian to a height of about 500 feet above the sea-level. From the old tower on the summit you can well see Biarritz and its lofty light-house, and the long sandy beach fading away in the extreme north-east towards Arcachon.

The harbour of San Sebastian is unsafe and shallow. The fish is excellent.

To return the same evening to Biarritz, you can either dine at the table d'hôte of one of the hotels at six o'clock, or at the *buffet* of Hendaye at eight o'clock, as the train from

Spain stops an hour there. You reach Biarritz at ten o'clock P.M.

Should you wish to drive all the way from Biarritz to San Sebastian, better sleep in the latter place, to avoid a drive of almost 80 miles on the same day. The high road not following the railway line, will now be described.

Leaving Biarritz by the road which leads to the railway station, you meet, just before this station, the majestic but formal road from Paris to Madrid. Take it (right). Four miles from Biarritz will place you on the hill of *Bidart*, a gay village, where you enter the Basque country. Then you descend, and climbing another hill, you soon reach *Guétharry*, with its milk-white Basque houses, two small hotels, a modest sea-bathing establishment, and a sandy little harbour. Fine seaview.

(It is five miles by the beach from Biarritz to Guétharry, a weary walk along the sands. Ophite and strange fossils are found in the rocks. You have to cross two streams.)

After Guétharry the road is perfectly straight for four miles, but *La Rhune* and other mountains are always in sight.

St. Jean de Luz is ten miles from Biarritz

(see Chap. VIII.). Follow the road to Spain. Two miles farther you pass close to *Urtubie*, a "modernized" old manor, belonging to the De Larralde family. Wellington and other great men slept there. Hilly country. A very short mile beyond you cross the village of *Urrugne*, with a sad inscription on the clock of its church, meaning, "*They all wound; the last one kills.*" You then ascend a hill, carried by the Allies in 1813, and with a splendid view of sea and mountains. In 1793 there was also severe fighting here. Ruins of redoubts.

Leaving on the right the railway and *Hendaye* (see above), you descend towards the west, facing the glorious hills of Spain, where the *Haya*, or "*Trois-Couronnes*," overtops all others. (South; see above.)

At length you come to *Béhobie*, the last town in France (17 miles from Biarritz), with two hotels, and on the right bank of the Bidassoa, which separates the two kingdoms. Half of the bridge belongs to France, and the other to Spain.

On the right is the celebrated but insignificant island, *des Faisans*, where, in 1659, the marriage settlements of Louis XIV. were signed by Cardinal Mazarin and Don Luis de Haro. A little pyramid stands on it.

Two miles from Béhobie take you, through a swampy but well-cultivated country, to *Irun*, where you join the railway route described above. And beyond Irun the road always follows the same tract of country as the railway line, the distances being nearly the same (37 miles both ways from Biarritz to San Sebastian).

CHAPTER X.

DAX, BUGLOSE, AND THE LANDES.

DAX is a small town of not quite 10,000 inhabitants, 31 miles (by rail) north-east of Bayonne, on the river Adour, and just an hour from Bayonne by rail. It was well known to the Romans, and called by Cæsar *Aquæ* (waters); hence "Dax." Its old ramparts are certainly of Roman origin.

Hotels: de l'Europe, and de France. Omnibuses at the station.

Bull-ring and cathedral. But the celebrity of Dax is due to its waters, and its mud-baths. One of the springs, remarkable for its abundance as well as for its temperature (158° Fahr.), is constantly covered with clouds of vapour, like the boiling mouth of a small volcano. In general, the Dax waters are used for rheumatism, especially in spring.

A very rich rock-salt mine, near the town, became three or four years ago the property of a celebrated English "savant," Mr. Maxwell-Lyte.

All the environs of Dax are full of thermal springs.

Roman mosaics and aqueducts have also been found quite near the town, and in it.

Steamers have ceased to run on the charming river Adour.

Buglose is a village, five miles north of Dax, but not on the Paris road. A station has that name on the Bordeaux and Dax Railway; but it is a mile and a half from the famous monastery. Some trains, however, at certain times of the year, stop at Buglose itself, where there are several little inns.

A Catholic need not be told what gives such interest to this otherwise unknown little village, lost in a wilderness of silent pine-forests and sand. It was within a few miles of it (at *Poueij*) that St. Vincent de Paul was born in 1576, and miracles beyond dispute have more than once hallowed the soil of Buglose.

Buglose is only five miles from Dax, where you can get any number of vehicles to carry you to it. Taking the Paris road for two and a half miles without any objects of interest, you then leave it and turn to the left, where you behold the cupola of the *Poueÿ* church, whose altar stands on the spot where St. Vincent de Paul was born. This beautiful building is well seen from the train as you go to Paris (right-hand side), at two miles after the Dax station. There is a Lazarist convent at Pouey, and opposite the church stands the majestic oak under which the great Saint, nearly 300 years ago, meditated in his boyhood. There is also a school, and a large hospital for old and invalid persons. Relics are shown of St. Vincent, who died in Paris in 1660.

From Poueÿ, the Buglose road goes nearly three miles through a gloomy pine-forest. And here I cannot do better than quote Mr. Shyne Lawlor ('*Pilgrimages in the Pyrenees and Landes*'), in whose poetical pages heart and intellect always go together.

" On the confines of the Landes and Chalosse, in the parish illustrated by the birth of St. Vincent de Paul, and in the middle of the sands, stands an ancient shrine, venerable in the traditions of the country and the faith of its inhabitants. Countless pilgrims have knelt before it in bygone times, and their number has not diminished in the present day. Few spots are more favourable to meditation and prayer. The only noise that intrudes upon the peaceful retreat is that of the tread of pilgrims, the song of psalmody, the lowing of the herds, or that melancholy and indefinable harmony which the pine-forest sends forth as it replies to the breeze. To the north and east of the chapel, plains of sand, covered by a low heather, spread to an unlimited extent: to the west are visible the vast forests of Marensin: in the distant south, the horizon is bounded by the rugged peaks of the Pyrenees, and by the fertile hills of Chalosse, watered by the winding Adour. On one side nature is all severe—arid sand, solitary steppes: on the other, she reigns over graceful sites, pleasant valleys, and grassy fields. Above this varied landscape towers Our Lady of Buglose, invoking upon it the blessing and protection of Heaven." ('*Pilgrimages*,' &c., page 567.)

The origin of the Buglose pilgrimages is uncertain; but centuries ago they already took place. See the lovely statue of the Blessed Virgin, seated on a throne of marble. The graceful attitude, harmonious proportions and tender expression of this admirable statue all combine to render it a masterpiece, due probably to the early period of the Renaissance. In all fairness however, it must be admitted that the present statue has not been proved to be the same as the one which rendered Buglose famous, before even the Huguenot wars. (See Lawlor, pages 569 and 570.)

The Oratory having been sacked in 1570, by order of Jeanne d'Albret, the Catholics concealed their dear statue in a morass, where it lay fifty years, and was at last found again by shepherds, or rather by one of their oxen; hence *Buglose* (Greek *Bous*, "an ox," and *glossa*, "tongue").

The present church is very grand indeed (Romanesque style). The pilgrimages take place on Pentecost Mondays. Here also Lazarists are found, and an asylum for aged and infirm priests. In 1856, there was a superb gathering, numbering no less than 600 priests; and in 1866 also, for the coronation of the statue.

Several trains stop daily at the Buglose station (one mile and a half distant); but when pilgrimages take place, and in the month of May, they stop at the monastery itself.

There is a strange and solemn harmony between the shrine of Buglose and the *Landes* scenery. The Landes are, on the whole, an awful wilderness, where a hundred miles can be travelled in a given line, on white sand forming great waves, and through endless pine-forests, mixed with cork-trees, twisted like demons. Except the wind, and the roar of the sea, nothing is ever heard in those deserts, though here and there you meet shepherds walking on stilts; they can thus go seven miles an hour. It is an unhealthy and swampy land, with dismal lakes, which become seas after the autumn rains; pines and poplar-trees emerge everywhere from the waste of waters, where hills form islands. For weeks after a flood, travelling in some parts of the Landes is all by water. In summer the white sand reverberates an Indian heat; and even then the soil is often treacherous, for there are pools beneath, where you sink through the sand.

The inhabitants are far too badly fed to be anything but wretched; the water is

Dax, Buglose, and the Landes. 115

impure, the land swampy, and the best thing they eat is maize.

Still the Landes are a rich country, thanks to the tar, or essence of turpentine (*résine*), extracted from those millions of pines. But the tree must be at least fifteen years old before it can produce it. Immense fortunes were made in this apparently useless country, during the American war; and some landlords own whole territories, worth 10,000*l.* a year, or even more. Their greatest enemy is *fire;* there are fearful conflagrations. Besides, sandstorms in the Landes are a serious affair; they amount to a real danger, though the sand-hills (*Dunes*) are nearly stopped now by the plantation of the pine, whose roots harden and fix the sand. But a few years ago, the sea used to encroach on this unhappy coast at the rate of from 60 to 70 feet a year! the sand-hills moving on towards the east like waves.

It is indeed a strange country, unlike any other part of Europe, and well worth a visit.

CHAPTER XI.

CAP-BRETON.

CAP-BRETON (*Caput Bruti*) is a village of 1300 inhabitants, in the Landes, 13 miles north of Bayonne, and rather more than a mile from the ocean. It is in a very swampy, although sandy country, mostly covered with great pines.

Better drive all the way from Biarritz (18 miles), unless you take the early morning train from Bayonne to Bordeaux, as far as the *Labenne* station, only four miles from Cap-Breton, where, in this case, you must remain till the evening.

Taking the Paris road, north of Bayonne, you first go through a populous and well-cultivated country, with gay villas, gardens, and fields on both sides, speaking of wealth, comfort, and civilization. But beyond the village of *Tarnos* (three miles from Bayonne), culture and civilization both disappear, the wilderness begins: pines and twisted cork-trees replace poplars and oaks, and you enter the almost boundless solitudes of the *Landes* (Chap. X.) where the sea-breeze howls night and day through the lofty pines. Here and there, however, the depressing monotony of the landscape is still broken by small tarns, as motionless as the Dead Sea, whilst in the extreme distance (S.E.) you get glimpses of snowy peaks.

Labenne (8½ miles from Bayonne; 13½ from Biarritz) is a station on the Bordeaux railway line. There used to be a lake (*Orx*) to the east of it, covering thousands of acres till a few years ago: but the whole place was drained, and not a trace of it is left.

After crossing the village of Labenne (half a mile beyond the station), and admiring its pretty church, you leave the Paris road to your right, and go due north towards Cap-Breton, on a much less formal and narrow road, between sand-hills of every size and shape, looking like huge waves. The sand is almost snow-white, and throws out an intense heat in summer. Still, some verdure is left, in the shape of ferns and pines. *Cistus* is abundant. Not a house is seen for four miles, till you reach

Cap-Breton, one mile from the sea, and on a sort of stream (the Boudigau), in colour more like beer than water. Little boats ascend it with the tide. You can breakfast at the Hôtel *Marin*.

This village was once very important, when the capricious river Adour here fell into the sea. But a fearful storm, 300 years ago, having swollen the Pyrenæan torrents to such an extent that they almost deluged all the Bayonne country, this irresistible irruption of waters again opened the natural basin of the Adour, by forcing the sand on both sides, and it left Cap-Breton for Bayonne. But before that, its bed had changed many times, and this restless river most probably ran into the ocean at Cap-Breton in the thirteenth century; later it went still farther north. By this now almost empty village one hundred ships were once anchored.

By crossing the Boudigau, and walking west for one mile over vine-covered sand-hills (producing the well-known *vin de sable*), you reach the Atlantic, under whose blue waters opens the gulf, or submarine valley called *Fosse de Cap-Breton*. Whilst on both sides of this deep gorge there is shallow water everywhere, the soundings give 200 fathoms over the *Fosse*, at less than a mile from land. It is supposed to run from east to west under the Atlantic for about seven miles, its width being from two to three. The sea is quite smooth over the *Fosse*, even when it boils on both sides of it. Still, it is full of currents.

Due north of Cap-Breton, two short miles distant, see the strange lake *Hossgort*. The sand, silence, and pines which surround this blue sheet of water (a mile and a half long), remind you so vividly of Australia or Canada, that you cannot realize you are still in Europe. (Do not get lost in the pine-forests upon the right of the lake.)

From Cap-Breton to Dax, 27 miles: good carriage-road.

LAC D'YRIEU.

A charming and easy excursion from Biarritz. You can drive the whole distance (14 miles). Go to Bayonne (five miles), and take the Paris road, as in the preceding section. At about 200 yards before the railway crossing, near the *Labenne* station, you turn off to the right, in your carriage, plunging into a grand pine-forest. A mile over sand takes you to Lake d'*Yrieu* (14 miles from Biarritz). The nearest village to it is *Ondres* (two short miles). There are dense woods round the lake, whose undulating banks rise in some places to about 100 feet, all covered with "jungle," and on whose still waters foliage everywhere droops in graceful festoons. It seems asleep in a cradle of leaves and flowers. The Pyrenees stand out clear in the distance (80 miles, and more). Observe, to the south-east, the proud fork of the *Pic du Midi de Pau* (9793 feet).

In the heat of summer, there is no better place for picnicking.

CHAPTER XII.

SARE AND ITS CAVES.

Sare is a large village, to the east of *La Rhune* (see Chap. XIII.), and almost due south of Biarritz, distant 18 miles by the woods of *Othecara*, and three miles less by *Arbonne*; but the latter road is detestable for carriages, the former very good.

After crossing the Biarritz railway station, you ascend a rugged and steep hill to the east, and then, leaving on your right (south) the Arbonne road, very bad for carriages, you continue for two miles to the east. The conical and conspicuous mountain which rises in the south-east, to the height of more than 6000 feet, is the *Orrhy*, the highest of the Basque hills (see Chap. XVI.); it is 45 miles distant.

At four and a half miles from Biarritz you must turn sharply to the south (right), and passing the château and village of *Arcangues*, from whence is a beautiful view of the Basque plains and Pyrenees, you soon enter a wilder and most hilly country, where the road, ascending, descending, and always winding, nearly doubles the actual distance. In fact, the whole distance between Biarritz and Sare is, as the crow flies, only 11 miles, although you have to go 18. When you are about nine miles from Biarritz, all traces of culture disappear, not a house is in sight, and you enter the great wood of St. Pée for three miles, going up and down, and in endless semicircles, between small oaks and gorse, whose yellow tints redeem the ugliness of the barren and brown moors stretching between the trees.

At 12 miles from Biarritz you fall into the Arbonne road, mentioned above, and three miles shorter, and, emerging from the forest, you descend (south-west) a long hill facing the La Rhune mountain (2920 feet). The village of St. Pée now appears below, with the fields bordering the *Nivelle*.

St. Pée (2600 inhabitants; several inns) is 14 miles from Biarritz (11 by Arbonne), 13 from Bayonne, 8 from St. Jean de Luz, 7 from Espelette (Chap. VII.), and rather more than 4 from Sare.

Sare and its Caves.

St. Pée has many old and picturesque Basque houses, and a good church.

To go to Sare, you start south, cross the *Nivelle* (which falls into the sea at St. Jean de Luz), and then gradually turn round towards the south-west, through a hilly and very green country, with the massive *La Rhune* straight before you.

You scarcely know when you enter *Sare*, so widely scattered are all its houses. It contains between 2000 and 3000 inhabitants. There is a comfortable inn, or small hotel, in the same building as the *Mairie*. There also you are sure to find a guide and candles, to visit the Sare caves, of which there are at least three very fine ones, the best of all being the one visited, in 1858, by Napoleon III. and the Empress, and opening south of Sare (four long miles), under the northern, or French side of the *Pic Atchuria* (2500 feet).

The church of Sare is both large and pretty, like most of the Basque churches.

To go to the grotto of Atchuria, or of *Lesia*, take a boy and candles, and give him 50 sous. You can drive two miles towards the grotto, and ride the whole way. There are ponies at

Sare. You go south, and after two miles, leaving the high road, you have only to follow up *ad libitum,* but always going up and down, the right bank (left side) of a stream which is one of the many sources of the Nivelle, and issues from the cave of Lesia itself. The country is dismal, but the Basque hills south of you form a noble line, although almost treeless. Four long miles from Sare take you to the gloomy mouth of the *Lesia* grotto, forming a regular and splendid arch, at least 40 feet in height, and running far away, as level as a floor, into the unknown depths of the *Atchuria* peak, on the summit of which is the Spanish frontier. In entering the cave, observe on the right an oval slab, commemorating the Imperial visit of 1858; and on the left, at a certain height, a mass of maiden-hair fern, looking lovelier still with such darkness near it.

There are numbers of other openings on the sides and *over* the main cave, which is composed of two stories, communicating with each other by steep and muddy "couloirs," where a few steps are cut to help ladies. But if once lost, even with a candle, in this mysterious maze, or system of grottoes running towards every point of the compass, and containing very deep pools, there would be little chance of escape. It is one of the most wonderful and one of the largest caves in the Pyrenees.

A clear streamlet gushes out of it, forming one of the numerous sources of the Nivelle. Bullock-carts have travelled a great way under the lofty vaults of the Lesia grotto, which is not half explored as yet.

The gloomy little village whose church is well seen to the east, in the middle of hills and moors, is *Zugarramurdy;* it is in Spain, though on the northern side of the Pyrenees, and on the banks of a river which enters France immediately. Here, as in many other places, the *natural* boundary (division of waters) has been sacrificed, in favour of Spain, to political considerations. But Zugarramurdy is too dirty to inspire any jealousy.

There are countless caves in this region. One to the east of the Lesia one, and only ten minutes' walk from it, with a very narrow opening, is very grand indeed. Further still to the east, and near *Urdax,* in Spain, there is a third, with a torrent running through it, and plenty of stalactites.

About three miles east of Zugarramurdy lies *Urdax* (in Spain also), with a few trees, and what was once a monastery. Gloomy church.

West of the Lesia cave, and on a *col* between the peaks of *Atchuria* and *Ibantelly*, see a line of lofty trees. Here are the *Palombières* of Sare. Huge nets are stretched in the autumn between these trees to catch ringdoves, in their annual flight from the north, across the Pyrenees. They never come with a westerly wind. (For more details, see Germond de Lavigne's '*Biarritz*.') It is a pretty walk of four miles from Sare; there are a few *cabanes*, or inns, near the summit.

N.B. — Five short miles east of Sare, and on the right bank of the Nivelle, is the village of *Ainhoa*, the last in France, on the Bayonne and Pamplona road. Inn, *Opoka*. It is situated on a well-cultivated and healthy plateau, between 400 and 500 feet above the sea-level, and west of the *Mondarrain* peak (Chap. VII.). Pilgrimages on Whit Monday. Ruins of a redoubt;

curious church. Grand view towards the N.W., from the top of the hill on whose slopes the chapel stands. The Atlantic is in sight, and the Biarritz light-house, &c. Fine place for sketching, though there is little shade; chestnut-trees here and there. The Spanish frontier is only two short miles south of Ainhoa, at the junction of two torrents which are the real source of the Nivelle. Ainhoa is 17 miles from Bayonne; excellent road.

From Sare you can drive back to Biarritz by Ascain (N.W.) and St. Jean de Luz, the distance being nearly the same (19 miles). It is five miles from Sare to Ascain, over a wild *col* about 1400 feet above the sea-level, and N.E. of *La Rhune*, of which you never lose sight. The road is both narrow and bad, but never dangerous; slopes gentle.

From Ascain to St. Jean de Luz it is four long miles, by the right bank of the Nivelle; 10 miles more take you back to Biarritz (see Chap. VIII.).

A wretched diligence, like an old and broken box, leaves Bayonne for Sare three times a week, in the afternoon, starting from the "Hôtel des Pyrénées," south of the town, in a dark street falling into the Rue d'Espagne.

It was by the side facing Sare that the allied armies under Wellington attacked and took *La Rhune* in October, 1813, with a loss of 1600 men. (See Napier, book xxii.)

For the fighting on the Nivelle, see Napier, book xxiii., chap. i.

CHAPTER XIII.

ASCENT OF LA RHUNE (2920 FEET).

IT is very easy to do this in one day from Biarritz; and any one after spending an hour in it, is sure to know La Rhune by sight: what Mont Blanc is to Chamounix, La Rhune is to Biarritz. It rises nobly, a few degrees west of south, at a distance (mathematically speaking) of 11 miles; but in reality, from Biarritz to the top you have to go 18 miles, of which you can drive 14 if you ascend by *Ascain* (north of La Rhune), or else 18 if you go by *Sare* (see preceding chapter), which is due east of it. Better go up one way and down the other, sending on your carriage from one village to the other. The ascent by Sare is longer, but less steep. Both at Sare and Ascain there are inns for breakfast, and generally ponies for ladies who prefer ascending on horseback; but sometimes none are to be found.

If you ascend by Ascain, leave Biarritz towards eight o'clock A.M., and drive to *St. Jean de Luz* (10 miles; see Chap. VIII.), whence you can either go by boat up the Nivelle with the tide to Ascain, or drive to it by the right bank, always facing La Rhune, which forms an imposing mass. The country is charming, Indian-corn, meadows, and woods alternating with rugged little cliffs, quite yellow with gorse.

It is a little over 14 miles from Biarritz to Ascain, where you can get guides (5 fr.) if you want them, and breakfast at the inn *De la Rhune*, near the church. Do not leave Ascain later than 12 o'clock.

Two hours from here will take a *man* to the summit; but a lady takes three. There is not the slightest difficulty anywhere, and you cannot even get lost (save in a mist) on these absolutely bare slopes, where scarcely anything grows but ferns; although La Rhune was once covered with woods, which were either burnt, or cut down for ship-building. It is now bald as a skull.

Seen from Ascain, a great ravine, generally dry, seems to split it in two for half of its height; and by far the shortest way to the summit is up the left bank (right side as you go up) of this rocky gutter. But it is easier to leave this on your left, and ascend S.S.W., instead of due south. The slopes are much gentler, since bullock-carts ascend half of La Rhune by the blood-red road you see winding up to the right of the *Huaïtz* torrent, under the doubtful shadow of stunted little oaks.

An hour's good walking takes you to a solitary house, with seven oaks to the right (or west) of it; and here you reach an undulating and shadeless plateau, covered with ferns and furze. After passing a few "cabanes," you go straight to the peak, rising abruptly before you, due south, and without a tree. Very gentle zigzags, good enough for ponies, will easily lead you to the summit.

If you go by *Sare* (18 miles from Biarritz; see Chap. XII.), you can ascend on foot, and steering west, by the hideous gorge which on its eastern side also tears La Rhune in two parts. But on horseback you must follow a track, well seen from Sare, which ascends W.N.W., on the northern slope of the smaller of the two ridges (the right one) which here descend from the summit. There is a most conspicuous little house (well in sight of Sare) which you must pass. After two hours of monotonous climbing, you fall into the Ascain track, on the plateau described above. On the whole, the ascent of La Rhune is gentler by Sare, but half an hour longer than by Ascain.

The view from this summit (2920 feet) may without hesitation be called one of the most magnificent in Europe, combining a huge extent of sea and plains, with an almost endless line of peaks.

All the Bay of Biscay is there under your feet, as on a map, from the Arcachon sands to beyond Bilbao: in clear weather it is as blue as the Mexican Sea, and the absence of ships makes it look infinite. To the north-east, the emerald-green plains of the Adour, glittering with rivers, and dotted all over with villas, or populous and snow-white Basque villages, carry the spectator's eye or imagination to the distant and still richer valley of the Garonne. Far away to the east, the central Pyrenees whiten the sky with their snows, and the *Pic du Midi de Bigorre*, through 90 miles of space, appears as plain as possible. Southeast and south of La Rhune, it is a strange chaos of barren mountains, sun-burnt and almost repulsive; but dear to the poet or historian, by their memories, and the noble or cruel deeds they have been witnessing for such numbers of centuries, since Charlemagne first rendered them famous. An Englishman ought to carry Napier's 'Peninsula War' to the top of La Rhune, which was taken by its eastern side (October 1813), after hard fighting, and with a loss to the Allies of 1600 men. Ruins of a redoubt are still seen on the summit, where you also find traces of a chapel and " Hermitage," which was a school for the Sare boys before 1793. They used to spend a week up there.

A modern and ugly obelisk commemorates the late Emperor's ascent. Woodcocks and partridges are common on La Rhune, and the ferns are beautiful. The rocks are puddingstone and red sandstone, and coal has been found.

On the slopes of La Rhune, vestiges still exist of a camp, called " Camp de la *Baïonnette*," where it is said the bayonet was first used by the Basque soldiers in one of their battles with the Spaniards; having run short of cartridges, they fastened their formidable knives to the muzzle of their guns, thus inventing the bayonet.

PART II.

EXCURSIONS REQUIRING SEVERAL DAYS.

CHAPTER XIV.

GROTTO OF ISTURITZ.

It is 30 miles from Biarritz to Isturitz, by Cambo and Hasparren (see below); a little less by Bayonne and Hasparren (27 miles); in either case you had better sleep out one night, either at Cambo or at Hasparren. You can drive both ways.

The village of Isturitz is two miles to the north of the Bayonne and St. Palais road. Leaving Bayonne in a south-easterly direction, between the Nive and the Adour, you pass *St. Pierre d'Irube* (one mile and a half), beyond which you enter the Basque country, and a very hilly region, where woods now and then alternate with great moors. This is the road to *St. Palais.*

Hasparren or *Hasparr*, is a Basque town of

more than 5000 inhabitants, and containing a whole population of shoemakers. Great cattle markets. Over the main gate of the church observe a marble slab with four Latin verses, of which the meaning is much discussed. This Roman inscription dates from Adrian (?), A.D. 117. Fertile hills, rising to about 500 feet, almost encircle Hasparren. It is exactly 15 miles from Bayonne, and consequently 20 from Biarritz.

Following up the road to St. Palais, through *Bonloc*, for about five miles beyond Hasparren, you then leave it and turn to the left (north), on a by-road, where you soon discover a half-ruined tower on the top of a hill. Under this tower runs the celebrated grotto of Isturitz, through granite and limestone. It divides into many branches, and forms a regular chaos of rocks, with quantities of beautiful stalactites. *Under* the cave runs the torrent of Arberoue, which reappears at the surface a little farther north, near the village of Isturitz. In certain floods the torrent rises to the level of the grotto and flows through it.

The hill of Isturitz is pierced with caves, like a honeycomb.

Should you prefer going by Cambo, you had better sleep there; in which case the second day's drive will represent about 40 miles.

From Cambo to Hasparren it is seven miles, through a hilly and very rich country. At Hasparren continue as above.

From Hasparren to *St. Palais* it is 18 miles, over hills and moors. (See Chap. XVI.)

St. Palais is consequently 38 miles from Biarritz, passing through Hasparren.

LOYOLA.

1st. *By Zumarraga.*

Take the Madrid express (which passes the Biarritz station at about one o'clock P.M.) as far as San Sebastian, where you arrive at three o'clock. (See Chap. IX.)

The line beyond this becomes a piece of wonderful engineering, an endless succession of tunnels and bridges, especially of the former. It is a long, continual rise along the banks of the rapid *Oria*. The first town of importance is *Tolosa* (8000 inhabitants), a clean, well-built and busy Basque town, 47 miles from

Biarritz. Hôtel de las Diligencias. It is in a charming valley, near the junction of two rivers, the Azpiros and the Oria. Church of Santa Maria. Over its portico there is a colossal statue of St. John the Baptist.

Beyond Tolosa the line goes through four tunnels, and crosses the Oria no less than fifteen times in nine miles! After *Beasain* (56 miles from Biarritz) there are nine tunnels in succession and four crossings of the Oria, besides a superb iron viaduct, 1000 feet long, over the fertile valley of *Ormaïsteguy*. The four stone piers supporting it are 120 feet high. Again you cross six more tunnels before reaching Zumarraga! In all, between Irun and Zumarraga, there are nineteen tunnels in 45 miles, and a rise of nearly 1200 feet. Still, this is as nothing compared to the line beyond (towards Madrid), which has to go through fourteen more tunnels before reaching its greatest altitude (2000 feet) on the Cantabrian Pyrenees!

Zumarraga is a village of 1400 inhabitants, standing at an elevation of nearly 1200 feet, on the banks of the river *Urola*, flowing north, and separating it from *Villareal* (1000 inhabitants). It is 65 miles from Biarritz, and the one o'clock express from Paris arrives here at 4.40 P.M. At 5.30 a diligence leaves for *Azcoïtia* (eight miles, 1s. 8d.); take it, leaving the Madrid line. After crossing the Urola on a stone bridge, you go through a hilly country, on a good road, running northward, along the waving banks of the river. Eight short miles will thus take you to *Azcoïtia* (5000 inhabitants), on the left bank, in a wooded little valley, and at the foot of the *Izarraiz*. There is a fine church and an hotel. One mile, across fields and gardens, takes you to *Loyola*.

2nd. By Zaraus.

Leave the Biarritz station, either by the early morning train, reaching San Sebastian at 8.10 A.M., or else by the 1 o'clock P.M. express, reaching San Sebastian at 3 o'clock P.M. Two diligences leave San Sebastian daily for *Zaraus*, one at 11 o'clock A.M., the other at 3.30 P.M. The distance is sixteen miles; time, two hours and a half; price, five shillings. Better hire a carriage.

You leave San Sebastian, going westward, through a charming and fertile country, where you follow the coast. Eight miles take you to *Usurbil*, on a hill; fine church.

Then the road is often cut out of the solid rock, before *Orio*, where you cross the Oria on a fine bridge. Hilly country. Sixteen miles from San Sebastian, the traveller reaches

Zaraus (1300 inhabitants), a beautiful sea-bathing place, with a grand sandy beach, a healthy climate, handsome villas, and pretty hills with chestnut-trees. Hotel *Atristayne*.

Here cross a ridge (S.W.), and then descend into the *Urola* valley, with villages on both sides.

Santa Cruz de Cestona is a large village, one mile from the baths of *Cestona*, where there is a very good hotel (eight miles from Zaraus). Waters good for rheumatism. Boats on the Urola, and mules for mountain explorations. Better sleep here.

Azpeitia (13 miles from Zaraus) contains upwards of 5000 inhabitants. Posada Nueva. A wall surrounds it; see in the church the silver statuette of St. Ignatius de Loyola.

A mile beyond it (30 miles from San Sebastian) is the *Santa Casa* and convent where this great saint, the founder of the Jesuits, was born in 1491. You have green hills and woods all round you, and the clear Urola looks asleep as it winds across the lovely vale of *Iraurgui*.

The *church* of Loyola, one of the richest and handsomest in Spain, was built by the Roman architect, Fontana. Its proportions and symmetry are beautiful. The cupola (70 feet in diameter) is built of the peculiar granite called *ophite*, found in abundance in the neighbouring hills. The portico is adorned with black and highly-polished marble, jasper columns, grand lions, &c. Above the main entrance, observe a white statue of St. Ignatius. Once inside the church, gloomy marbles, alternating with red and white ones, almost make you shudder, as if night were rushing upon you; the altars are splendid, and wherever you look you see marble, alabaster, jasper, &c.

There are two towers each, 125 feet high, and the total height of the dome, cross included, is 166 feet. All the lines of this remarkable building are of exquisite grace.

An *hotel* stands near the monastery, which was built in 1683.

The church was not yet finished, when the Jesuits had to leave Spain, under Charles III.

There is a great pilgrimage yearly to Loyola (July 31st). Dancing and bull-fights, &c.

Biarritz to Loyola and back takes two short days, and you have thus the choice of two ways; but the best plan is to hire a carriage at San Sebastian.

CHAPTER XV.

BILBAO.

1st. *Along the Coast.*

Go by rail to San Sebastian (Chap. IX.), whence to Bilbao, by Guernica, 85 miles. It is a diligence road, but badly kept, especially near Bilbao.

As far as *Zaraus*, see Chap. XIV. (16 miles from San Sebastian). From here two and a half miles take you to *Guetairia*, a small harbour, with a Gothic church. After three more miles you reach the Urola, which you cross in a boat, and come to

Zumaya (1700 inhabitants), an old but very clean town (Roman). Sea-bathing place. You now go due west, along a hilly coast, and reach

Deva (29 miles from San Sebastian), a pretty town, as large as Biarritz, and very full in summer. It stands between the sea and high hills. Cross the Deva by boat.

Motrico (two miles from Deva) is famous

for its fish and vineyards. Here the hills are wooded. Two long miles from Motrico, out of sight of the sea, take you to

Ondarroa (33 miles from San Sebastian), at the end of an almost land-locked little bay, with wooded hills (chestnuts and oaks) on all sides. Iron mines. Road very bad.

Lequeitio (39 miles from San Sebastian) is a fortified town, with a beautiful view. From the top of the hill called *Alto de Lequeitio*, Biarritz is in sight (distance, 45 miles). There is a fine bridge, of one very bold arch. (2500 inhabitants.)

Now the road strikes inland (S.W.), through a very hilly country, for about 15 miles, to

Guernica (54 miles from San Sebastian), a Basque village, "where," says Murray in his 'Guide to Spain,' "was held the Parliament of Basque Senators. . . . . This congress originally sat under the overspreading canopy of an ancient *oak*, which the town still bears on its shield. . . . . The French republicans cut down, in 1808, the time-honoured oak of the free Basques, a tree which was very old even in 1334!"

Thirty-one more miles over a fertile, and

here and there wooded, but rough country, take you by *Mundaca, Bermes, Munguia,* and at last *Begoña,* to BILBAO (85 miles from San Sebastian).

2nd. *By the Loyola Valley.*

As far as *Azpeitia* (29 miles from San Sebastian), see Chap. XIV. Two miles farther south is *Ascoitia* (see Chap. XIV.), on the wooded banks of the Urola. Ascend (N.W.) the *Azcarate* ridge (1000 feet above the sea), and then descend into the *Deva* valley. You come to

Elgoibar (22 miles from Zaraus, and 38 from San Sebastian), near the saline springs of *Alzola.* Elgoibar contains 2000 inhabitants, has a good inn, and mineral waters.

You now cross a high table-land, with immense oaks and beeches. Pass *Eybar* (4600 inhabitants).

Durango (51 miles from San Sebastian) has 2600 inhabitants, and lies in one of the most beautiful plains of Biscaye. Very old church, and pretty walks. The road improves. Sixteen miles from here to

BILBAO (67 miles from San Sebastian by the Loyola valley).

3rd. By Villareal and Vergara.

Go by rail to *Zumarraga* (65 miles from Biarritz), separated by the river Urola, from *Villareal* (1000 inhabitants), whence you drive over a ridge to *Vergara* (eight miles), Hotel de las Diligencias, and de la Posta. (4000 inhabitants.) Vergara is surrounded by mountains. In the San Pedro church, see the fine statue of the Agony of Christ, by Montañes. Here the Carlists capitulated, in August, 1839. Diligences every second day to *Durango* (14 miles), whence to *Bilbao*, 16 miles.

Distance from Zumarraga to Bilbao, by Vergara, 38 miles.

4th. By Rail all the way.

Take the *early morning* train from Biarritz to *Miranda* (132 miles, seven hours). You cross the Cantabrian Pyrenees near *Otzaurte* (78 miles from Biarritz), at a height of almost 2000 feet. Very wild scenery. You also go through *Vitoria* (110 miles from Biarritz), the capital of Alava, with a population of 18,710 inhabitants. Hotel de Pallares. Battle of Vitoria, June, 1813.

Miranda has 3000 inhabitants, and is on the Ebro. Fonda del Norte. Here you leave the

Madrid line, and have to wait an hour before starting for Bilbao (65 miles north).

The journey by rail from Miranda to Bilbao is one of the most wonderful in Europe, the scenery being almost Alpine, and the line ascending in one place (*Inoso* station) to 2163 feet, whence it descends, in about 40 miles, to the level of the sea, by the most eccentric curves. It was engineered by Ch. Vignolles, C.E.

The most remarkable town you pass is *Orduña* (Inn, Aduana), with 3240 inhabitants. Beautiful excursions, trout fishing, and superb fall of the *Nervion*, forming a grand cascade, 700 feet high. (See Murray's Hand-book to Spain.)

Orduña is 42 miles from Miranda, and 23 from Bilbao, which is finally reached (four hours from Miranda) after crossing a beautiful plain.

BILBAO is thus 197 miles from Biarritz: time, 11 hours.

5th. By Sea.

Steamers leave Bayonne two or three times a week for Bilbao (83 nautical miles). The passage takes about ten hours, including a stoppage at San Sebastian. Price, 1st class, 21 fr.

BILBAO, capital of Biscaye, contains about 35,000 inhabitants, and stands on the right bank of the Nervion, eight miles from the sea. It is a thriving and commercial town, almost surrounded by Scotch-looking hills, forming the very last headlands visible from Biarritz towards the west. One of the four bridges is beautiful. Promenade del *Arenal*, on the river-side. Bull-fights in summer (August). Cock-fights.

Hotels: de las Navarras: della Antonia: del Boulevart, &c., &c. Good club-house.

Boats and omnibuses every hour to *Portugalete* (seven miles), the port of Bilbao, and a fashionable sea-bathing place. Grand sea-view, near the church. Three miles from Portugalete are the famous iron mines of *Somorrostro*.

PAMPLONA.

1st. By Rail.

The distance from the Biarritz station to Pamplona is 116 miles. You first go 83 miles on the Madrid line, as far as *Alsasua*, whence

33 miles to Pamplona. By leaving Biarritz station early in the morning, you reach Pamplona at 3.40 P.M. (See map.) For description as far as Alsasua ("buffet"), see page 138. From here to Pamplona the line crosses a hilly and well-watered country, with high peaks in the distance.

2nd. By Coach, over the Col de Maya.

It is a beautiful drive of 65 miles from Bayonne (67 from Biarritz). Before the opening of the railway by Irun, diligences used to run regularly between Bayonne and Pamplona; but although they still go sometimes, they are no longer to be counted upon. They left from the "Porte d'Espagne" (south end of Bayonne), and performed the journey in one day, stopping for breakfast at Elizondo. Better take a carriage at Biarritz, and either sleep at Elizondo (30 miles), or have a change of horses there.

You cross the Pyrenees east of *La Rhune*, the picturesque and most conspicuous summit rising nearly due south of Biarritz.

(Another carriage-road, but much less frequented, though equally interesting, leaves

Béhobie, the last town in France as you go to Madrid (see Chap. IX.), and goes due south to Pamplona along the right bank of the Bidassoa. It is as long as the other. (See map.)

To go by the Maya col, leave Biarritz by the Cambo road (see Chap. VII.), and follow it until it divides (13 miles), at a mile beyond *Ustaritz*. Here, leaving on the left the well-known Cambo road, you go to the right, and begin a long but gradual, and more than once interrupted, ascent of eight miles, through a very wild country, resembling a desert of ferns, though here and there it is wooded.

After *Espelette* (16 miles from Biarritz, see Chap. VII.), you go up and down for three miles and reach *Ainhoue*, the last village in France. Custom-house. It is a most unnatural frontier, the division of waters being several miles farther south; but this anomaly is common in the Pyrenees, and generally to the advantage of Spain. A bridge on the Nivelle (two miles beyond Ainhoue, and 21 miles from Biarritz), forms the frontier.

(For description of Ainhoue, or Ainhoa, see Chap. XII.) Look N.W. towards the sea.

You now reach *Urdax*, in Spain. Posada de la Toreta. (See Chap. XII.) It was by Urdax that Don Carlos both entered Spain (1834) and left it (1839) a fugitive.

Gently rising on and between barren summits, with a grand view behind, towards the plains of Bayonne, you make your way to the Col de *Maya* (26 miles from Biarritz; under 1600 feet high).

In 1813 the *Col de Maya* was carried by the French, after a bloody engagement; but their defeat at *Sorauren* compelled them to abandon it. "So dreadful was the slaughter at Maya, that it is said the advancing enemy was actually stopped by the heaped mass." (*Napier*.)

Beyond the Col, you go down on the southern slopes of the Pyrenees to the village of *Maya*, and a mile lower down you will see to the west the bare summit of *Achuela*, or *Atchiota*, where King Joseph spent his last night in Spain. You cross several streams, which, soon uniting, form one of the sources of the Bidassoa (Chap. IX.).

"These bleak and exposed heights," says Murray's Guide, "were held, in July, 1813, by

General Stewart, when Soult attempted to relieve Pamplona."

Elizondo (1300 inhabitants, and 30 miles from Biarritz) is the capital of the very fertile valley of *Baztan*, which runs N. and S. for 24 miles, and contains about 8000 inhabitants. There is a tolerable inn at Elizondo (de Estevan Fort) where you can sleep. This village was several times taken and lost by the Carlists.

As you descend the Basque valley of the Baztan, the mountains become less bleak; you find woods of oak, beech, and chestnut, cottages, and clear streams with trout. Before *Almandoz* (40 miles from Biarritz, and 1360 feet in height) you cross a marble bridge, and then travelling due south through dense forests of beech, passing the *Venta de Velate*, once a Templar chapel, you once more begin to ascend in zigzags until you reach the

Port de *Velate* (3350 feet), beyond which the descent is rapid, for in 11 miles you go down 1750 feet to *Olague*. Road is cut through the rock.

You now leave the Basque country, and the type of the natives is quite altered.

Sorauren (62 miles from Biarritz), although only a very small village, has a great name in history, as it was there that in 1813, Soult was beaten by the Duke of Wellington after a very sanguinary conflict, which cost the French 3000 killed or wounded, and the Allies about as many.

From hence, on foot or riding, you might go (N.E.) to *Roncevaux* (16 miles), whence Soult made a furious, and for a time successful, descent on the British army (1813).

PAMPLONA (Pompeiopolis) is a wonderfully old city, rebuilt by Pompey nearly 2000 years ago! Capital of Navarre, it now contains 23,000 inhabitants. Living is cheap, but the hotels are bad (del Infante, del Florentino, &c.). It is a well-built, but not very strongly fortified town, standing on a height in the middle of a rich plain. The citadel is to the south-west of the town.

The cathedral, built in 1397 (light Gothic), has beautiful cloisters, and an enormous bell in one of its towers. It is outside the city.

Bull-fights in July and August.

There is a grand and most extensive view from the Promenade de la Taconera.

CHAPTER XVI.

A RIDING OR WALKING TOUR OF ABOUT TEN DAYS IN THE FRENCH BASQUE COUNTRY.

HAVING now described in detail the popular places round Biarritz, we shall ask the reader to follow us in a longer, and more or less circular, tour of about 230 miles through the Basque plains and mountains, extending from Biarritz to near the *Vallée d'Aspe*, which runs south and north to *Oloron*, and touches the country already described in my previous work, '*Pau and the Pyrenees.*'

If on foot, a knapsack is enough for this tour. A passport is useful.

FIRST DAY.— *Biarritz* to *Bidache* (26 miles). Go to Bayonne (five miles).

From Bayonne you must take the road to Oloron (60 miles; diligences). You go out of Bayonne by its south-eastern suburb, between the Nive and the Adour, and after passing *St. Pierre d'Irube* (one mile and a half), enter the Basque country. Go east. The country is both rich and hilly, and very populous. At a distance of nine miles from Bayonne you pass the village of *Briscous*, a few miles south of the Adour; but before reaching it, see on the left, in the Ardanabia valley, the celebrated salt works of Briscous. There are five large factories (rock salt, very white). You ascend to Briscous (1620 inhabitants). Continue east, up and down, and over two rivers (the second called the *Joyeuse*); the Pyrenees (S. and S.E.) look very grand.

At 11 miles from Bayonne, you leave on your right (south) the road leading (two miles and a half) to *Labastide-Clairence*, a Basque village, with a colony of Jews.

(*N.B.*—Near this village, on the Ayherre territory, and close to a house called Lucuya, "*lucus*," are still seen, in a gorge once wooded, the stones of a *Cromlech*, where the Druids used to perform their rites.)

Bardos is 16 miles from Bayonne. Curious church, and château de Gramont, on a hill. Traces of camps in the neighbourhood. You now descend towards the pretty river *Bidouze*.

Bidache is a Basque town on the left bank of it (21 miles from Bayonne, 26 from Biarritz). See the ruins, on a bold hill, of the castle of *Grammont*, burnt in 1793. The Dukes of Grammont are buried in the church. Bidache was taken by assault and sacked by the Spaniards in 1623. Three miles N.W. of Bidache, the smooth and transparent river Bidouze, softly flows under the picturesque ruins of *Guiche*, well seen from the Bayonne and Pau Railway. Some trains stop there (*Came-guiche*; 15 miles from Bayonne).

Bidache reminds one of Henri IV. and the beautiful *Corisande*, Countess of Guiche, whose attachment to him lasted as long as her life; but whom he refused to marry, although the promise to do so was written with his blood. This unhappy and forsaken beauty died in 1620.

Cardinal Mazarin and Napoleon III. were also visitors to Bidache. South of it, one of the countless roads of the Basque country runs to *St. Palais* (15 miles), over wild and almost uninhabited moors. (See map.) (Bidache is only six miles from *Peyrehorade*, a railway station 21 miles from Bayonne.)

SECOND DAY.—Bidache to Salies, and thence to Sauveterre (in all, 21 miles). Going nearly due east, through *Came,* you reach (eight miles from Bidache) the village of *Labastide-Villefranche,* with an awful dungeon; and here, leaving on the right (south) the road to St. Palais (11 miles), go north-east, and cross the *gave* of Oloron, which falls into the gave of Pau at Peyrehorade, about eight miles to the N.W. Observe ruins of fortifications. A short mile will then take you to *Caresse,* whence it is four good miles (east) to

Salies, a town of over 5000 inhabitants, famous for its salt spring. Several hotels. Its population is steadily decreasing, by emigration to America. There are traces of camps, or *casteras* in the neighbourhood. Excellent hams, called " Bayonne hams."

Salies is only five miles from *Puyôo* and from *Baigts,* two stations on the Bayonne and Pau Railway, 30 and 34 miles from the former.

From Salies to Sauveterre (south) it is seven miles, over a wide hill.

Sauveterre (1500 inhabitants) lies on the right bank of the gave of Oloron. Ramparts in ruins. It was besieged by the Prince of Orange (see Ad. Joanne's 'Itinéraire des Pyrénées'). The church is worth seeing. For the fights in this district (1814), see Napier, book xxiv. You are in Béarn, not in the Basque country, which only begins a few miles southwest of Sauveterre, on the St. Palais road.

N.B.—Sauveterre to St. Palais is 9 miles (S.W.). St. Palais is a Basque town of 1683 inhabitants (*Donapalesa*), in the charming valley of the Bidouze. Hôtel de la Poste. There was a mint there formerly. It is 20 miles from St. Jean Pied de Port, and about the same from the station of Peyrehorade, on the Bayonne and Pau Railway, 21 miles from Bayonne.

Sauveterre to Mauléon, up the Saison Valley, is 14 miles. *Mauléon* is also a Basque town, of nearly 2000 inhabitants. Two hotels (*de la Maréchale* and *Habiague*). It is 27 miles from Orthez (a station on the Bayonne and Pau Railway), 9 from Tardets, 24 from St. Jean Pied de Port. (*Maleo, Malus leo.*) It is on the turbulent stream *Saison*, and is the capital of the Souletains (*Sibilates* of Pliny). See the ruins of its once fortified castle, on a very steep hill (right bank of the stream). There was fierce fighting there during the wars of religion. There is a curious church at Mauléon, with three little spires in a line, perhaps meant to symbolize the Trinity (?) This architectural arrangement is very common in Basque churches.

At Mauléon were held the "General Assemblies," or "States" of Soule.

It was the birth-place of Henri Spondé, a famous Calvinist, born in 1568, who became a Catholic, and finally bishop of Pamiers; also of Oyhenart, Basque historian.

The Pyrenees here become mere hills, and die away on the plains. The drive from Mauléon to Tardets (9 miles south) is beautiful. Observe the beds of ancient lakes, of which the absence is now so conspicuous in the Basque country.

THIRD DAY.—Sauveterre to Oloron, along the gave (23 miles). Always follow up the left bank of the river, which you only cross at Oloron itself. The villages you pass are almost countless, so populous is this interesting and fertile valley.

At 10 miles from Sauveterre, just before crossing *Sus*, you can turn to the left, and cross the gave to *Navarreinx*, a once fortified town, where you had better stop for breakfast (25 miles from Pau, by *Monein*, and a very pretty drive). From here to Oloron (in fact, from Sauveterre also) there is a road on either bank. If you choose the left bank, you leave on your right, a few miles before Oloron, the village of *Montmour*, with an old tower attributed to the Sarrasins; and you at last reach Oloron by its western suburb of Ste. Marie.

During the whole of this journey, which, from Biarritz, a good pedestrian can easily perform in three moderate days' walking, you never cease to see the Pyrenees on your right, on a line parallel to your own, and gradually increasing in height from west to east. Very often glimpses may be had of the graceful monarch of these regions, the Pic *d'Anie* (8216 feet), the loftiest in the Western Pyrenees, and of very easy ascent. It rises south of *Navarreinx* (30 miles. See *Pau and the Pyrenees*). West of this peak the Pyrenees begin to sink, but very gradually; and nothing in its way can be more beautiful, especially on a summer evening, than this jagged line of blue or snowy mountains, often black with forests, standing like a wall between Spanish Navarre and the Basque plains, and dipping towards the west, with the sun, into the Atlantic.

You can drive the whole of the journey just described.

Oloron (*Iluron*), though beyond the limits of the Basque country (see map), is often supposed to mean in Basque "Town of good waters." It is a gay little town, of 9000 inhabitants, 20 miles south-west of Pau, and has a good hotel (Condesse). Diligences to Pau daily. Two noisy and clear Pyrenæan torrents, or *gaves*, meet here, under the grassy hill where the town proudly stands, only a few miles from the line of lofty peaks whose rocks and woods seem to steam in the sun, and already rise to thousands of feet above the plains.

Oloron was long a Bishopric. It is now a thriving town, although it was plundered and half ruined, in 1694, by the Spaniards. Great markets. It is two miles long, being very narrow. See the *Ste. Croix* church, built in 1080.

Diligences to Orthez, St. Palais, St. Christau, Bédous, Pau, &c., &c.

FOURTH DAY.—Oloron to Tardets. (Diligences as far as *Aramits*, nine miles.)

Leaving Oloron in a south-westerly direction, on a capital carriage-road, you first proceed through a very fertile but flat country, with the blue Pyrenees standing up on your left, like a bold and rugged wall, almost covered with boundless forests abounding in game. Along the road there are poplars, small oaks, heath, meadows, and villas; and a little beyond, the plain begins to undulate as you approach the Pyrenees, bleak little hills rising here and there like waves.

Six miles take you to a bridge, where you cross the *Vert*, a clear and modest stream descending from the south, down the *Barétous* valley, famous for its cows, its scenery, and the many traces the Sarrasins have left in it. The view from this bridge, looking south, is quite Swiss-like.

After *Féas* (six miles and a half) you soon reach *Aramits* (nine miles from Oloron).

Now you leave the plains, and enter a very hilly country, facing abrupt and rocky peaks to the south, where the *Anie* (8216 feet), and its almost always snowy summit, stands out most boldly.

South of *Lannes* (11 miles from Oloron), there are, in the autumn, huge nets, or *palombières*, for catching wild doves, as they fly over the Pyrenees.

Then you gently rise to the Col de *Lapixe*, and go down a long and steepish hill to the village of *Montory*, beyond which you enter the Basque country, with its mountains rising here to about 4000 feet. Ferns everywhere, green slopes, and white farms scattered all over them.

Montory has iron mines, and looks wealthy

(15 miles from Oloron). Beyond this you go west, on a more level road, to *Tardets* (19 miles from Oloron).

As you enter Tardets, the "Hotel des Voyageurs" is on your left. The scenery is singular, but picturesque; all the lines are as broken and tortuous as in a volcanic country. To the west, conical and almost countless little hills rise in confusion, and far beyond, the Pic des *Escaliers* (4900 feet, W.S.W.) rears its brown and barren slopes, whilst to the south, 12 or 13 miles distant, the peaks of *Ste. Engrace* reach 6000 feet, and even more.

Immediately round Tardets the land is fertile, being watered by the foaming waves of the *Saison*, but the circle of hills beyond is rather bare.

The climate is strange and changeable: hot south winds are frequent in autumn, and bring rain; but the north wind often blows above it, and the clouds are seen to struggle between them.

Tardets (1000 inhabitants) has imposing and handsome houses, and a pretty new church. Here was born Chaho, the elegant Basque historian.

Living is very cheap: five shillings a day suffices for luxury.

N.N.E. of *Tardets* there rises a hill called *La Madeleine* (2700 feet), and well worth an ascent. A poor chapel stands on the top, and it contains a marble slab, with a Roman inscription. There are yearly pilgrimages.

To ascend *La Madeleine* (four miles to the top), you first rise N.E. on a cart-road for about 45 minutes, then continue N.W. on a barren and windy moor for half an hour. The view from the summit is grand indeed, although you cannot see the sea. The plains are boundless, and you can see very clearly, not only the *Pic du Midi de Pau*, but also that of *Bigorre*, fully 60 miles away. Even the humble hills of *Lourdes* are quite plain (50 miles due east). But the *Anie* (8216 feet), being so near (S.E.), is the real monarch of this grand chain. The Pic d'*Orrhy* (6660 feet), its rival, also towers very nobly in the S.W.

You can descend westward, more abruptly, and thus save a mile. Here are magnificent chestnuts. But the ascent of *La Madeleine* is deceptive as to distance. It is much farther than it looks.

in the French Basque Country. 165

Altogether, Tardets would make excellent head-quarters for good pedestrians. It is nine miles from *Mauléon*, a town north of it: diligences daily. Two short miles north of Tardets, in the lovely valley of the Saison, on the left of the road, stands the château of Count de Montréal. Built in 1662–4 by M. de Trevilles (one of the heroes of Dumas's *Trois Mousquetaires*), and once visited by the Duchess de Berry, it is called *Trois-Villes*, and is a charming place, surrounded with trees and fields, where the *Saison* winds and roars between a double row of wild hills, whose bleak points appear above the trees. In fact, on all sides, mountains, great or low, frown upon the lawns of Trois-Villes, its trees, and its rustic bridges. In the south, the view is almost Alpine.

N.B.—From Tardets to *Roncal*, a Spanish village due south of it, on the other side of the Pyrenees, it is nine hours' walk or ride over the *Col de la Pix* (4600 feet), exactly due south of Tardets: this is midway. Pretty church at Roncal (500 inhabitants), where, in the eighth and ninth centuries, the Moors suffered bloody defeats.

FIFTH DAY.—Tardets to Larrau and the Pic d'Orrhy.

It is 11 miles from Tardets to Larrau (S.W.), the last village in France on that side, and you can drive it; the last mile only being difficult for carriages.

First go south on the right bank of the Saison. The scenery is rather tame and uninteresting, but at *Licq* (four miles) it improves. Here the torrent forms a small cataract. A mile beyond Licq the valley divides, the left branch running up to *Ste. Engrace*, a village of 1200 inhabitants, most romantically perched high up in the Uhaïtxa valley. You must ride or walk to it (two and a half hours), and the only dwelling you pass is the custom-house. The natives are all Basques, though very fair, says M. Ad. Joanne. According to the Rev. Haristoy, already quoted (Chap. IV.), "the Ste. Engrace monastery and abbey were already flourishing in the eleventh century. The monks fulfilled, among other duties, that of guiding travellers through those wild and inhospitable regions. The Basque country had many of these institutions, half hotels, half monasteries. Tardets (in Basque, *Atharatce*, 'a refuge for strangers') owed its origin to one of them. Of the monastery of Ste. Engrace nothing now remains but a handsome church of the purest Romano-Byzantine style."

(*N.B.*—It is only five hours' walk from Ste. Engrace to the top of the Pic d'*Anie* (S.E., 8216 feet), which you ascend by its western side. View splendid.)

Continuing your journey to Larrau, and leaving on your left the Ste. Engrace muletrack, you come to the junction of both torrents (Uhaïtxa and Saison); this "meeting of the waters" is five miles from Tardets. Crossing the Saison on a handsome bridge, and looking up (S.E.) towards the *Arlas* summits (6700 feet), you now enter a narrow, tortuous, and densely-wooded gorge, and gradually get imprisoned in a perfect maze of middle-sized mountains, with cheerful houses perched at every height on their slopes or summits. In fact, the gorge becomes so contracted, that you can easily throw a stone across it; there is just room for the road and torrent, which is half bridged over by the straight branches of mighty chestnuts and oaks, under whose leaves the furious stream boils, and whitens every rock. Occasionally, but only for a few moments, you get glimpses of high peaks to the south (*Bimbalette*, 6000 feet).

At a mile before Larrau there is a steep

ascent, detestable for carriages, and turning towards every point of the compass. After passing a wretched inn, you go westward, observing on the right (north), on the other side of the torrent, a broken and jagged precipice rising to nearly 1000 feet.

At last you reach the plateau of *Larrau* (11 miles from Tardets, and about 2500 feet above the sea-level?). In the west, modest hills undulate, emerging from a sea of forests (*Iraty*).

Larrau is a neat and compact village of 1200 souls. The inn (*Topino*) is not at all bad. Iron-foundry two miles to the west. Waterfall of *Holsat*, two hours to the east, in the forest of the same name.

The *Pic d' Orrhy* (6660 feet), well seen from the Bayonne country, can easily be reached in three hours (on foot) from Larrau, but is not seen from it. It rises to the S.W. of it. It is a noble peak, though so humble, and chamois are found on its rocks. Slopes of grass will take you to the top by its southeastern side. You first ascend from Larrau to the *Col de Larrau* (4500 feet, S.W.), passing before the *St. Joseph* chapel. Riding or walking, two hours will bring you to the *Col*, whence to the top of the Orrhy it takes a good hour. The Atlantic is quite visible from the summit.

N.B.—A very easy descent of two hours, in a southwesterly direction, would take you from the Col de Larrau to the Spanish village of *Ochagavia* (1300 inhabitants), at the foot of the *Musguilde* mountain, where stands an *hermitage*. Wretched inns; but lovely view south, down the Salazar Valley. Ruins of two castles. (See Ad. Joanne's admirable 'Itinéraire des Pyrénées.')

SIXTH DAY.—Tardets to Ahusky. It is about 12 miles. Direction, west. You can drive for four miles, and ride the rest of the way. Start W.S.W. from Tardets, crossing the Saison on a pretty bridge, and facing the *Pic des Escaliers* (4900 feet). After passing several villages, better leave the carriage-road (three miles) on your left, and begin to ascend on the right, on barren, stony slopes, rather bad for a horse. You thus follow the left bank (right side as you go up) of a gloomy gorge. Houses and culture gradually disappear; it is like a moor of Donegal. Nothing is heard, and there is no water; ferns extend everywhere. Two hours and a half (walking) from Tardets will place you on a *col* with beech-trees; and there you meet a track coming up, on the right, from Mauléon (same distance as Tardets). In the forests stretching below on that side gipsies are found.

Go to the west, in a level and pretty straight ravine, without a torrent, between a double row of fern-covered hills. See a *cabane*, then another, on your right. It is a strange and dreary place, 3000 feet above the sea-level. There is not a sound, and no view; you go from east to west through a kind of dismal gallery, all brown with ferns. At last, at the western end of it, opens a *col*, or depression, to the right of which are seen five or six small houses, one of them rose-coloured, which is the inn of Ahusky. What a relief, what a blessing in bad weather! for there is not a tree or a rock near, beneath which you could get shelter. Height, 3000 feet. It is nearly four hours' walking from Tardets to Ahusky, most unquestionably one of the strangest places in all the Pyrenees. The wilderness is appalling. But you can get a bed and a dinner in the inn, even in mid-winter, although the snow is sometimes five feet deep! North of the inn

in the French Basque Country. 171

there is a little hill, almost 4000 feet above the sea-level; on a clear winter day the Atlantic is visible from this point (40 miles away, N.W.). From the inn itself the view is very grand also towards the south and east; the *Pic des Escaliers* especially (4900 feet) looks very bold and majestic (S.S.W.), rising in solemn solitude, behind long and waving slopes, all covered with ferns. Wolves and bears are common in these windy deserts, as the shepherds know but too well.

Left of the *Escaliers* there is an easy passage to Larrau (three hours); there is much going up and down, but no climbing to speak of.

Under your feet, to the south-east, runs a valley with dense woods, rushing streams and verdure; and due south of Ahusky, only seven miles distant, the *Pic d'Orrhy* proudly stands, humiliating all its neighbours. To the S.S.E. there is a long line of peaks (*Arlas, Anie*, &c.), generally covered with snow.

Far away to the east you can just see the *Bigorre* mountains (80 miles).

On the whole, a few days may be pleasantly spent at Ahusky in a bracing and splendid climate. There is a famous spring within a hundred yards of it; you can drink with impunity whole bottles of this most peculiar water, fifty glasses a day being a common dose! It is good for fever, digestion, and the nervous system. It is said to bubble in the glass like soda-water (?).

A good pedestrian could walk in about eight hours from Ahusky to the Spanish village of *Ochagavia* (alluded to above), by penetrating through the magnificent forests of Iraty, probably the largest in all the Pyrenees. The direction is south-west, as far as the frontier, where you enter Spain by the *Port d'Aborreta* (4000 feet), west of the Pic d'Orrhy. Then you steer due south, and go down in three hours to Ochagavia. But no one, not even a member of the Alpine Club, ought to attempt this excursion without a compass and a map. Once lost in the forest of Iraty nothing but a compass could possibly save you.

Geologists ought to visit, near Ahusky, the deep natural holes or wells, beneath whose gloomy depths torrents are heard roaring.

N.B.—Biarritz tourists should certainly not fail to go to Ahusky, a curious place indeed, with much game, no summer heat, and all the necessaries of life. It is a little over 50 miles south-east of Biarritz, passing by Cambo and St. Jean Pied de Port; you might sleep in both places comfortably.

in the French Basque Country. 173

SEVENTH DAY.—Ahusky to St. Jean Pied de Port. This is a journey of 18 miles; and you can ride the whole distance.

From Ahusky go west, on a mule-track, ascending a little. You soon find yourself on a brown and gloomy wilderness of heather, with a few rocks only to break its distressing monotony. It is indeed a melancholy place in bad weather. There are deep holes right and left, with water running in. Towards the north-east you catch a few glimpses of great blue plains in the distance, the only thing which can remind you of your height (3000 feet). Look back (S.E.) at the majestic peak d'*Anie* (8216 feet). Wolves are common here in autumn and winter.

Westward you now see three bare little summits, rising a few hundred feet above your own level. Steer to the left of the middle one, the highest, *Aphanicé* (4200 feet). An hour from Ahusky will make you reach three good *cabanes:* plenty of rocks; no trees. Grand view below, west and north-west. You begin to descend in earnest, first west, then northwest: bad road for mules. Once on the western side of the rocky arête of the Aphanicé, you get a most extensive view towards the north-west, where a valley, studded with villages, and green as emerald, runs far away fully 2000 feet under your own level. Its trees, torrents, and fields form a lovely contrast with the solemn and bare summits around you. But St. Jean Pied de Port is not yet in sight. The soil here is very ferruginous, and quite red. Do not go down straight into the gorge below you; it is longer. Keep to the left, on an undulating, weather-beaten, and round ridge, where you descend very gradually, by a succession of terraces going due west.

Passing under a few chestnuts, you come at last (2.30 from Ahusky) to the *Mendive* commune, where, on level ground, you meet a carriage-road.

(*N.B.*—From hence you might reach on foot, in eight short hours, the Spanish village of *Ochagavia*, already mentioned, by always going *south*, crossing the enormous forest of *Iraty*, then the torrent of the same name, and finally the almost unexplored, but humble, *Abody* mountains, south of which a short descent of about two hours would take you to Ochagavia.)

After *Mendive*, continuing north-west towards St. Jean Pied de Port, you pass near some unimportant iron-works, and reach the village of *Lecumberry* ("new house"). Decent inn on the left, opposite the custom-house. (Three hours from Ahusky.) Four miles more, on an excellent road, and through a beautiful country, like the hilly parts of Ireland, take you to *St. Jean le Vieux*, where leaving on your right the fine road to *St. Palais* (18 miles), you turn abruptly to the left (west). From here, two miles and a half will land you at St. Jean Pied de Port. (Observe on a commanding hill to your left the neat and imposing château d'*Irumberry*.)

St. Jean Pied de Port is a fortified little town of about 2000 inhabitants, almost surrounded with barren hills, and in the very heart of the French Basque country. It is only five miles from Spain. *Hotel de France.* The citadel is a strong one; the streets are very narrow, but clean. Three streams (or *Nives*) meet here. It only belongs to France since 1659, and was fortified by Vauban. See the church, and do not fail to taste the chocolate.

St. Jean Pied de Port is 40 miles from Bayonne, by *Irissary, Helette,* and *Attisane* (diligences daily); but only 35 by *Louhossoa* and

Cambo (carriage-road), and 42 by *St. Etienne de Baïgorry*, *Bidarraÿ*, and *Cambo*.

The diligences, which are wretched, leave Bayonne from the Hôtel des Basques, near St. André.

N.B.—From St. Jean Pied de Port to Mauléon it is 24 miles by the high road. Take the *St. Palais* road (N.E.). At five miles you cross *Lacarre*, where Marshal Harispe is buried. He distinguished himself at Jena, Friedland, Saragossa, and in 1814. At seven miles, after passing a little *col*, you go down (N.E.) through a dreary valley, to *Larceveau* (10 miles). Ruins of walls, destroyed during the wars of religion, says M. A. Joanne. Here leave the St. Palais road, and turn sharply to the south-east, ascending the *Bidouze* valley. Trees re-appear. The beautiful little river Bidouze springs from a grotto, five miles higher up. You soon leave it, after passing *St. Just* (13 miles), and rise to the left. You then reach a windy plateau, covered with ferns, and with a splendid view; the Pyrenees rise south to 6000 feet, and the sea, though 40 miles distant, is seen in the north-west. Now descend through a charming valley, by *Musculdy* (20 miles), to *Mauléon* (24 miles), for description of which, see above.

EIGHTH DAY.—St. Jean Pied de Port to Roncevaux is 17 miles (eight by carriage).

This is part of the projected road from Pau to Pampeluna. Passing by the church at St. Jean Pied de Port, and there turning to the right, you rise gently on an excellent road, along the right bank of an insignificant but clear little river, or "nive," called *Arnéguy*. (See high up on the hills to the left, the old and shorter track to Roncevaux, by the *Bentarte* col.)

The banks of the torrent of Arnéguy are green, wooded, and populous: but the hills above them are uninteresting and barren.

At four miles, you pass the village of *Benta*, with very white houses. Here you are still in France, but the left bank of the torrent becomes Spanish. The Arnéguy, imprisoned between slopes of intense green, becomes more noisy, and large chestnuts soon make their appearance above.

At the village of *Arnéguy* (five miles from St. Jean Pied de Port: about fifty houses) you cross the stream on a wooden bridge, and enter Spain. Almost the whole population is composed of smugglers. The road now ascends in long zigzags to

Valcarlos or *Luzaïde* (eight miles from St. Jean Pied de Port), a long village with a few very handsome houses. The carriage-road, for the present, stops here: and you must walk or get a mule to go to Roncevaux.

In the Bathing Establishment (*d'Hydrotherapia*) you can live comfortably. There is also an inn beyond the church (left of the road). See the *Plaza " de la Constitucion,"* a pompous name indeed, considering it is only built on one side!

The scenery is tame, but pastoral; there are hills, verdure, and shade almost everywhere. The climate is excellent, not too hot in summer. You are in Spain, but the opposite bank is still in France. It is only at two miles beyond Valcarlos that both banks are Spanish.

The mule-track you now follow is in a lamentable condition, but the scenery improves, and you enter forests of colossal chestnuts, worth measuring: there are none like them in all the Pyrenees. After a few miles, the valley stops against a *cirque*, or immense wall of hills, all black with dense forests, where a solitary house, white as a fresh flake of snow, alone glitters amidst the gloom. The road passes just under it, as it ascends the wooded cirque. But before beginning this ascent, your track divides. Go to the left, and here cross the torrent. (The track to the right leads in two hours to *Burguete*.)

As you ascend south in long, endless zigzags, under chestnuts and beech, on an atrocious road, the northern horizon becomes more imposing towards the lovely regions of Cambo and the Nive. But round you it is dark as night, under those massive trees where nothing moves or shines. After passing the white house mentioned above, which stands just midway up the hill, you must turn sharply to the left. At last you reach the

Col de Roncevaux (3700 feet, 16 miles from St. Jean Pied de Port), leaving on your right the crests of the *Lindux* (see below). There is a deserted chapel or *hermitage* on the top of the col, south of which the view is very strange. The whole country, as far as you can see, scarcely sinking below a level of 3000 feet, looks like a vast table-land, with wooded hills running everywhere on its surface like the Atlantic billows. The whole horizon seems one mass of forests, without a house in sight. But here and there a few acres of beautiful verdure shine in those enormous woods, and streams murmur, though you cannot see them.

The group of barren peaks east of the Col de Roncevaux is vaguely called *Altabiscar*.

Here the rear-guard of Charlemagne's army, retreating from Spain, was exterminated by the Basques in 778, and the brave paladin *Roland* (or Rotlandus) lost his life. In 1813 Soult crossed the col with a powerful force, and succeeded in rolling back the British troops towards the Spanish village of *Sorauren*; but here his advantage ended in a sanguinary defeat.

It was also through Roncevaux (says Murray) that the Black Prince led his legions in 1367, to the victory of Navarrete.

Chestnuts here disappear, or nearly so, and are replaced by beech-trees. You descend one mile, and suddenly find yourself at

Roncevaux (*Rossida vallis* in Latin, *Roncesvalles* in Spanish), a group of houses standing 3000 feet above the sea-level. Passing through the convent buildings, whose frowning and gloomy walls remind you of a fortress, you reach the inn, almost the last house on the left-hand side. Clean beds and good living, for a few francs a day.

Visit the church (Gothic) and the convent of Augustine monks, the cloisters, &c. The supposed boots, gauntlets, &c., of the great paladin, of Ariosto's hero, *Roland*, are shown in the sacristy.

This strange and imposing plateau is one of the least known regions in all the Pyrenees, although you could live there comfortably for months, avoiding the summer heats, away from all the luxury, necessities, tumult, and foolishness of crowded towns and watering-places. What a fine retreat for a philosopher!!

It is two short miles from Roncevaux to the village of *Burguete*, whence two roads lead to Pamplona; one for diligences (which start every morning), and about 30 miles long; another, much shorter, and more to the west, but only practicable for horses or mules (about 25 miles).

In round numbers, it is 50 miles from St. Jean Pied de Port to Pamplona (whence to Biarritz by railway, about nine hours. See Chap. XV.).

NINTH DAY.—Roncevaux to Aldudes and St. Etienne de Baïgorry (in all, 21 miles).

From Roncevaux, if you look to the west, you will observe a sharp little summit, overtopping the vast forests which girdle it; to the right of it lies the track to the Aldudes, a French Basque village. Take a boy for a guide as far as the *col* (one franc). Leaving Roncevaux in a westerly direction, by an avenue of ash-trees, see *Burguiete* in the distance (south), glittering in the sun, surrounded by a sea of trees. A compass and a map are extremely useful in these unfrequented regions. There is a tortuous mule-track which rises gently at first through the forest; you steer N.W., then W., after crossing a sluggish stream. It is a short and easy hour from Roncevaux to the *Col de Macharica* (3400 feet), a sort of wide ridge, covered with grass, and running south-west of the *Pic de Lindux* (4100 feet), on the summit of which a severe engagement took place in 1813, between Ross's column and Marshal Reille. "Brave men," says Napier, "fell on both sides; but numbers prevailing, these daring soldiers were pushed back again by the French."

From the summit of this much-exposed ridge, the view is striking towards France, where the peak of *La Rhune* (Chap. XIII.) appears to advantage in the north-west. Here again, as in so many parts of the Pyrenees, you are still in Spain, although north of the crest-dividing waters. Observe a green and grassy col far below you (N.W.); there you must go down through the forest, making a long semicircle to the right. You soon re-enter France, pass the custom-house, and go through a very open and rather bleak country, all torn with gorges and ravines, whence issue the sources of the Nive, which joins the Adour at Bayonne, after a course (almost due north) of about 50 miles. You stand hundreds of feet above the *right* bank of one of those torrents, which all unite their waters 2000 feet lower down. Once on the little col spoken of just now (45 minutes from the main ridge you passed), you cross a narrow spur, and suddenly find yourself on the *left* side of another gorge, and at a still greater height above the torrent. Here comes a steep descent, over hideous and large ravines, full of loose stones. Once on a level with the torrent, you pass a big house, re-ascend a little to the left, where you once more find culture—chestnuts and fields—and cross a second spur. The road improves, and you reach at last the right side of a third gorge, leading down in gentle slopes to the valley and village of Aldudes. There is a lovely view below (N.W.), where a line of white Basque houses stand sparkling in the sun, between meadows and poplar-trees, lining the cradle of the Nive. Everything breathes cleanliness, comfort, and happiness, not to say wealth.

See (north) a tall and brown mountain (4500 feet), the *Pic de Hausas*. The others are ugly, rounded, and vulgar.

Once upon level ground, the first village you reach is *Urepel* (three hours' walk or ride from Roncevaux): and here there is once more a carriage-road on the right bank of the Nive. (You must therefore ride or walk all the journey just described, from Valcarlos, through Roncevaux, to Urepel.)

Two miles and a half beyond Urepel, you enter the *Aldudes* (11 miles from Roncevaux). There is a good hotel south of the church, close to the bridge. 1226 inhabitants. A small "*cabriolet*," holding two passengers, carries the mails daily to *Irissary*, on the Bayonne and St. Jean Pied de Port road. The French and Spanish Basques often meet at Aldudes, to fight out the *jeu de paume*.

It is a long, straggling village, and, like most Basque villages, apparently endless. There is an easy mule-track, leading in three hours from the Aldudes to the Spanish village of *Elizondo* (N.W.; see Chap. XV.), over the Col de *Berdaritz* (2300 feet), carried by the French in 1794.

It is 46 miles from Aldudes to Biarritz, by Bidarray and Cambo, but only 40 by Elizondo and the Col de Maya (see Chap. XV.). To drive the whole distance you must take the former road, which is far more interesting.

On the hills south-east of Aldudes there are "*Pantières*" to catch ringdoves.

As you go on, you now fall into an excellent carriage-road, descending N.N.E. the valley of the Nive, alternately on either bank. The gorge is so narrow that it often becomes a mere ravine with a torrent, and it is easy to throw a stone across. Chestnuts, ferns, and rocks more or less adorn the conical and pretty little peaks rising on every side. The road is often red in colour, and winds like a snake. Five miles beyond Aldudes you pass a *foundry*, and some copper and silver mines, with upwards of fifty galleries or wells, often attributed to the Romans. See (east) the peak of *Adarca* (4300 feet). Cultivation improves as you approach

St. Etienne de Baïgorry, 10 miles from Aldudes, 21 from Roncevaux, 7 from St. Jean Pied de Port, 36 from Biarritz, by Cambo. 2500 inhabitants. Inn, *Bergugnan*, at the north end of the town, near the "jeu de paume."

During the last century, cannon used to be cast at or near St. Etienne. Antimony and iron are found in the neighbourhood.

The town is in a valley, as smiling and green as possible, but all the hills near it are bare and grey. It is the birth-place of Marshal Harispe.

A mule-track goes over the frontier, west of St. Etienne de Baïgorry, leading in three hours to the Spanish village of *Maya* (see Chap. XV.), whence to Biarritz it is 27 miles by carriage-road.

TENTH DAY.—St. Etienne de Baïgorry to Cambo and Biarritz (in all, 36 miles).

From Baïgorry you go down the left bank of the Nive; nothing very interesting; chestnuts, ferns, and modest hills. Seven miles place you at the junction of the Arnéguy and the Nive; venerable old bridge covered with ivy. A little farther on, the gorge opens upon the fertile plain of *Ossès* (2000 inhabitants). Here where the Nive, transparent as crystal, flows under a beautiful bridge, you leave the main road which goes N.E. to *St. Palais* (20 miles), and follow on the left the by-road crossing Ossès, on the left bank of the Nive. It is a carriage-road. At a mile beyond Ossès, you take the right bank. Pedestrians can follow the left bank all the way to Cambo, passing by the *Pas de Roland* (see Chap. VII.): it looks shorter, but it is scarcely so, on account of the continual ups and downs.

The river Nive, your companion, guide, and friend, is no doubt one of the most attractive of Pyrenæan torrents, and perhaps the purest and the most winding; you never know where it is leading you. When its waters are calm they are as translucid as glass, and as green as the leaves floating on their surface, for there can be no mud or deposits in that clear bed of rocks. But the Nive runs rapidly and madly sometimes, when choked between two hills, and shoots right and left like the wind or an arrow, throwing masses of foam upon its green or stony banks.

As you descend towards Bidarraÿ, observe bold peaks to the west, as bare as the sandy summits of the Red Sea. Spain is behind them. But your road is lined with chestnuts, poplars, Indian-corn, box-wood, and oaks. Ten good miles from St. Etienne de Baïgorry take you to

Bidarraÿ, the only filthy place I ever found on Basque soil. Avoid sleeping there. Fine old bridge. "Holy grotto" in the neighbourhood.

Bidarraÿ to Biarritz is 26 miles by Louhossoa, and carriage-road; not much less by the banks of the Nive and the *Pas de Roland*. (Chap. VII.)

Below Bidarraÿ the carriage-road continues down the right bank of the Nive for two miles, then it turns quite away from it to the right, passes over a little *col*, and beyond it, enters the Basque village of *Louhossoa* (manufacture of *Kaolin*, "porcelain clay"), five miles from Cambo.

At Louhossoa (two inns) you join one of the two capital roads from St. Jean Pied de Port to Bayonne; you turn to the left, go down a long hill, recross the Nive on a suspension bridge, and at last reach the village of *Itsatsou* (described in Chap. VII.), north of the Pas de Roland, whence, steering north, you will enter *Cambo* by its western side. Cambo is 21 miles from St. Etienne de Baïgorry, and 11 from Bidarraÿ.

For the road from Cambo to Biarritz (15 miles), see Chap. VII.

So here we are once more in beautiful Biarritz; and we re-enter it without that sadness which often falls upon the soul like a chain or a cloud, when we say good-bye to Nature and Freedom, two things so dear to travellers, and so hard to part with!

INDEX.

	PAGE
Abody	174
Aborreta	172
Adour	17, 22
Abusky	170
Ainhoa	126, 150
Alava	46
Aldudes	184
Alsasua	148
Altabiscar	179
Alzola	145
Anglet	41
Anie (Pic d')	160, 167
Aragorria	98
Aramitz	161
Arbonne	121
Arcangues	121
Arlas	167
Arnéguy	177
Ascain	130
Atalaya	14
Atchuria	123
Azcoïtia	139
Aspeïtia	140
Baigts	157
Baïonnette	133
Bardos	155
Barétous	162
Barre	27
Basques	31–68
Bayonne	16
Béhobie	107
Benta	177
Bernardines	26
Biarritz	1
Bidache	155
Bidarray	188
Bidart	106
Bidassoa	97
Bidouse	155
Bilbao	148
Bilsar	56, 77
Biscaya	43
Bonloc	136
Boulogne (Bois de)	27
Brindos (Lake)	29
Briscous	155
Buglose	110
Burguete	181
Cambo	75
Cap-Breton	116
Cestona	140
Chambre d'amour	24
Ciboure	93
Dax	109
Deva	143
Durango	145
Elgoibar	145
Elizondo	152
Escaliers (Pic des)	171
Espelette	85
Fuenterrabia	101
Guernica	144
Guétharry	87, 106
Guiche	156
Guipuzcoa	44
Hasparren	135
Haya	99
Hendaye	96, 97
Hossgort (Lake)	119
Iraty	71, 172
Irun	99
Isturitz	135
Itsatsou	83
Jaysquivel	102
Jeu de paume	49
Labastide-Clairence	155
Labenne	117
Lacarre	176
Landes	114
Lannes	162
Larrau	168

	PAGE
Lecumberry	175
Lequeitio	144
Lesa	123
Licq	166
Light-house	11
Lindux	182
Louhossoa	188
Loyola	137, 141
Luzaide	177
Madeleine (La)	164
Makila	58
Marbella	9
Marion (Lake)	30
Marrac	79
Mauléon	158
Maya (Col de)	151
Mendive	174
Miranda	146
Mondarrain	84
Montbrun	26
Montmour	159
Montory	162
Motrico	143
Mourisoot (Lake)	28
Navarra	43
Navarreinx	159
Nive	17, 187
Ochagavia	169
Oloron	160
Ondarroa	144
Orduña	147
Ormaistéguy	138
Orrhy (Pic d')	168
Ossès	187
Palombières	126, 162
Pamplona	153
Pasajes	103
Pas de Roland	83
Peyrehorade	156
Pouey	110
Puyòo	157

	PAGE
Refuge	25
Renteria	103
Rhune (La)	129
Roncal	165
Roncevaux	180
Roncevaux (Col de)	179
Ste. Engrace	166
Ste. Etienne de Baïgorry	186
St. Jean de Luz	86
St. Jean Pied de Port	175
St. Palais	158
St. Pée	122
Salies	157
San Marcial	99
San Sebastian	103
Santa Casa	140
Sare	121
Sauveterre	157
Socoa	92
Sorauren	153
Tardets	163
Tarnos	116
Tolosa	137
Trois-Couronnes	99
Trois-Villes	165
Urdax	126, 151
Urepel	184
Urrugne	107
Urtubie	107
Ustaritz	76
Valcarlos	177
Velate	152
Vergara	146
Vitoria	146
Yrieu (Lac d')	119
Zaraus	140
Zugarramurdy	125
Zumarraga	138
Zumaya	143

Lightning Source UK Ltd.
Milton Keynes UK
UKOW03f2331201014

240407UK00001B/81/P